# UNDERSTANDING AND LOVING A PERSON WITH

## NARCISSISTIC PERSONALITY DISORDER

# UNDERSTANDING AND LOVING A PERSON WITH

## NARCISSISTIC PERSONALITY DISORDER

*Biblical and Practical Wisdom
to Build Empathy, Preserve Boundaries,
and Show Compassion*

## STEPHEN ARTERBURN, M.Ed.
## AND PATRICIA A. KUHLMAN, M.R.C.

DAVID C COOK

*transforming lives together*

UNDERSTANDING AND LOVING A PERSON WITH
NARCISSISTIC PERSONALITY DISORDER
Published by David C Cook
4050 Lee Vance Drive
Colorado Springs, CO 80918 U.S.A.

Integrity Music Limited, a Division of David C Cook
Brighton, East Sussex BN1 2RE, England

The graphic circle C logo is a registered trademark of David C Cook.

Library of Congress Control Number 2017964690
ISBN 978-1-4347-1058-1
eISBN 978-0-8307-7272-8

Cover Design: Amy Konyndyk

Printed in the United States of America
First Edition 2018

3 4 5 6 7 8 9 10 11 12

020521

I pray that out of his glorious riches he may strengthen you with power through his Spirit in your inner being, so that Christ may dwell in your hearts through faith. And I pray that you, being rooted and established in love, may have power, together with all the Lord's holy people, to grasp how wide and long and high and deep is the love of Christ, and to know this love that surpasses knowledge—that you may be filled to the measure of all the fullness of God. Now to him who is able to do immeasurably more than all we ask or imagine, according to his power that is at work within us, to him be glory in the church and in Christ Jesus throughout all generations, for ever and ever! Amen.

—Ephesians 3:16–21

# Contents

# Introduction

If you are in a relationship with a narcissist, there are so many ways you may have been hurt by this person that few people would understand. And the sad thing is that the person who would understand the least is the very narcissist you care about. Most likely you were drawn to this person, as everyone else was, because when you meet a narcissist for the first time it feels as though it is all about you. You believed this person cared deeply for you and you were intrigued by the power and presence this person possessed. Quite frankly, when narcissists are doing what they know how to do best, they are not just charming; they are charismatic and appear to have everything and everyone under control. Seeing a narcissist in action is quite something to watch. In order to do so, you have to detach and distance yourself emotionally so that you are not in the whirlpool of manipulation that engulfs any and everyone who is unaware of what they are dealing with.

The irony, of course, is that none of this is a display of personal and relational mastery. It is, instead, a defective survival strategy that allows the person to exist on a day-to-day basis without having to feel the pain and hurt from whatever it was that happened early on that produced a deep, dark wound that has never healed. Just imagine the narcissist as a wonderful, loving person who connects with people in what seems to be a supernatural way but inside feels like an outcast, a reject, someone whom you would not like very much if you fully knew the person. That is fairly close to the experience of narcissists, but not quite. Not quite because they do a lot of things to deny the feelings of being emotionally and spiritually and relationally inferior to others. They are people who want you to know them and love them, but they are so afraid you would reject who they really are that they go to a lot of extremes to never let you in close enough to see the real person. They don't let you see it, and they don't even know who the real person is.

In the world of addiction, you might say that narcissists are addicted to themselves. They could attend meetings of *selfaholics anonymous* and fit right in from day one. But they would not want to go because they would not allow themselves to see who they are or who they have become. So they just keep on interrupting people, spewing negative emotions all around, and manipulating others to get whatever they can out of anybody who gets close. They think they are on top of it all and it would terrify them to know and understand that they are completely unaware of how they look to knowing eyes. In a very real sense, they do not know the pain they have caused. They may not even be aware they have a problem at all. It is just one of the realities that makes it so very painful to be in a relationship with a narcissist.

But the reason I am overjoyed you are reading this book is that there is hope for every narcissist. And there is hope for you. Transformation is possible for anyone who is motivated and willing to do whatever it takes to change and get better. I think this valuable book will help you help the one you love rather than make the wound worse or enable it to continue to control you and the narcissist. This could be the book you have been looking for or waiting for. I hope it is.

—Stephen Arterburn

# Preface

This is a book about hurting and hope. It is a book about broken-ness and healing. It is a book about pain and promises. And it is a book about captivity and freedom. Narcissism—the good, the bad, and the ugly—is what we will be addressing, along with how to live with people in our lives who are afflicted with it.

Thank you for choosing to read this work. We know that if you or someone you love is trapped in a relationship with a narcis-sist, you're feeling hopeless that life can ever change. You might be feeling so broken you can't imagine that the wounds inflicted by a narcissist can ever be healed. You have probably searched other resources in the hope of finding answers only to experience once again the pain of broken promises. And finally, you can't even imagine what freedom from pain feels like because you're stuck in a dark tunnel with no light at the end. If this is you, we're glad you're here.

Most good books begin with a story. I'd like to ask you to consider that the affliction of narcissism seems to have had its beginnings in a very old but important story. Our book begins with the greatest story ever told. It is God's story, and it touches all our lives. It is the historical tale of how all of humanity became separated from Him the moment sin entered the world. We'll talk about how we can choose to move through our brokenness and separation from God to a new life in Christ where all our sins are forgiven. God knew that we would suffer pain, heartache, temptation, and betrayal anytime we chose to be in relationship with other people. And God knew beforehand what each of us would face.

Because He loved us so much, He wanted us to love Him back. So He gave us the freedom to choose—to choose to love the world and everything in it or to choose Him through our belief in the atoning work of His Son, Jesus Christ on the cross.

The narcissist is a person who may appear connected to people and even to God—yet remains quite separated and independent from both. He, like the rest of us, experienced the same inner longing for connection at one time in his life. Yet many would describe him as quite disconnected from everyone, including his own emotional self. The narcissist rarely seems pleased or satisfied with the people in his life, and despite what he shows externally to those around him, internally, he's not even satisfied with himself.

In order to find hope again, you need to first identify how you lost it. Therefore, it's important to become aware of how narcissism first presented itself in the people you love. Then we'll explore how it has impacted your life as well as the lives of others on the periphery of the narcissist's circle. The narcissist operates in such a way that it often seems he sucks all the air out of the room. The cost is high when that happens to you. Get ready as others share their stories of pain and heartbreak at the hands of the narcissists affecting their lives. I hope you will be able to relate. I suspect you probably have stories of your own you could share.

To understand the narcissistic personality, we'll identify what makes it a disorder and examine a few key thoughts about how it came into being. I would suggest that the roots of narcissism can be traced to the original Fall of Man. We'll also address trauma in this book, both yours at the hands of a narcissist and the ways a narcissistic person may also have experienced trauma in his own life.

We'll discuss the kinds of help available to heal the wounds of the victim-survivor as well as treatment options to deal with the narcissist's co-occurring disorders. Keep in mind that we all have the freedom to heal. We must make that choice individually even though it may not be a simple or easy one to make. But as you will read, the narcissist's view of healing may be quite different from yours.

It will be especially important that you consider the person with Narcissistic Personality Disorder (NPD) to be someone who possibly, not by choice, has developed this destructive pattern of living as a way of defending himself against the exposure of his own vulnerability. Even he knows little about the depth to which his own life has been affected.

When people are born with various diseases and disorders, do we love them any less? Consider the diabetic spouse whose entire life can be affected by this life-threatening disease, not to mention how the lives of family members may be altered by the requirements of the diabetic's treatment regimen. If the diabetic is related to you, you don't have to like all his behaviors, particularly those that threaten to make the disease worse or even threaten early death and disability. But would you love him any less?

Or think about the alcoholic or drug-addicted person who steals, cheats, and lies to get his next drink or drug fix. Along the way, he victimizes family, friends, and complete strangers. You don't have to like, accept, or condone this deplorable behavior. In fact, you may need to protect yourself and others from the addict's destructive actions. Would you stop loving the addict if that person were your son or daughter? Of course not!

As you prepare to begin your journey to understanding narcissism, I want you to consider two important things. The first is that the stories and examples you are about to read may trigger painful memories of experiences you, too, have endured. Second, whether you can specifically relate to each story is not the most important thing. What might be most important is for you to reflect on your feelings and the thoughts you have about your own personal story. I hope you will gain new knowledge from what you are about to read, and I hope you will begin to see this complex disorder and the people who are afflicted with it in a whole different way.

The National Institute of Health (NIH) estimates that approximately 6.2 percent of the population suffers from Narcissistic Personality Disorder and that 75 percent of those afflicted are men. Narcissism falls on a continuum. It's often accompanied by co-occurring disorders such as alcoholism, drug addiction, sexual infidelity, and mood disorders. For ease of reading, I will be referring to the person with NPD by using the pronoun "he" since most people afflicted with the disorder are male.

Also, please consider that some facts and all names have been changed to protect the confidentiality of those who shared their stories.

Empathy and compassion for those afflicted with Narcissistic Personality Disorder is necessary for those of us who claim to be children of God. With God's strength operating in and through us, we can take back our lives and have great hope for a brighter future for both the narcissist and those impacted by his behaviors and distorted ways of thinking.

—Patricia Kuhlman

# CHAPTER 1

# It All Began with an Apple

Why, my soul, are you downcast? Why so disturbed within me? Put your hope in God, for I will yet praise him, my Savior and my God.

—Psalm 42:5[1]

This book is intended to help you understand the very specific nature of Narcissistic Personality Disorder. To see it revealed on a continuum from narcissistic traits and features to a full-blown, clinically diagnosable case of NPD may make it difficult at times to identify, particularly when additional co-occurring disorders are present. What we do know is that if you have picked up this book, you have probably been wounded by the person you love as he repeatedly belittles, discounts, betrays, and even lies to you for what seems like no understandable reason. Your relationship may be so out of control that you feel as though you've lost your sanity.

People with Narcissistic Personality Disorder may not realize there is anything wrong with their thinking or behavior. Symptoms differ, depending on where they fall on the NPD continuum. Generally though, people afflicted with this disorder have problems relating to others and handling stress, while strongly maintaining a self-image that differs from how others perceive them. Narcissistic Personality Disorder is now believed to play a significant role in each of the other personality disorders, which include: Histrionic, Borderline, and Antisocial personality disorders. Individuals in that particular group of disorders, called Cluster B, are characterized as possibly having experienced more adverse psychosocial experiences in childhood and exposure to more trauma and higher rates of physical abuse.

The representative stories presented here are composites created from real-life experiences of people who have lived with a narcissist or have been in a close relationship with someone who exhibits Narcissistic Personality Disorder (NPD). Maintaining the confidentiality of all the people involved in this project has been our goal, although as you read their stories, you may begin to believe that someone really does know and understand what you've been living with. Our attempt is to present situations that you may have heard about or have already experienced as you live with or closely interact with a person with NPD.

Some of the stories include situations involving verbal and emotional abuse, lies and betrayal of marital vows by infidelity, along with much more. In cases of toxic NPD, physical and sexual violence often occurs. However, our primary goal is to help you, the reader, begin to understand and learn from your experience while ultimately growing in empathy for the person afflicted with this very complex and damaging disorder. Listen closely as you review these pain-filled stories. Do not be surprised if you find yourself relating more than you might have imagined.

When Ella arrived on the doorstep of my psychotherapy practice, I noticed her moods shifted quickly from anger to tears. She
spoke so rapidly that it seemed she was afraid she wouldn't get to
tell all that was in her heart and mind. When she slowed to catch
her breath, she looked up and asked a pointed question, "Do you
think I sound like I'm truly crazy?" I quickly asked, "Has someone
been telling you that you are crazy?"

Ella sounded desperate. "Richard refuses to discuss any important matters with me—like finances, our adult children, even
planning for his pending retirement. He either creates a scene by
telling me I'm trying to control everything and then walks out the
door, or he yells at me saying, 'How many times do I have to tell
you these things? You may think you're a smart woman, but you
are dumb when it comes to common sense.'" Ella identified for
me that she had run a successful small business operation for years
that involved complex communication with others while helping
them work through their own life difficulties. "How can I possibly
be so inept in my marriage yet be a help to so many others?" was
the question that plagued her mind.

Ella continued trying to express herself by telling me the many
crazy-making behaviors that had happened over years of marriage
but were now escalating as she and her husband became empty
nesters.

"His latest crazy-making behavior is turning out the lights in
the bedroom or bath when he's done getting ready for work," Ella
related. "I've asked repeatedly why he does that when I'm standing
in the same room. He repeatedly denies ever turning out the lights
on me and chides me with his sarcastic cackle, saying, 'You know I

wouldn't do that to you.' He tells me I never said things that I know I've shared with him in detail, and he's always saying I'm the one losing my memory. His ultimate dismissal of me happens when he says, 'You're just crazy and I think you're losing your mind!'

"I know I need help, but I'm pretty sure I'm not crazy. I can't trust anything he says because he changes his mind later and feels absolutely no responsibility to let me know. He makes assumptions about me without asking me and acts on these like we talked it over. I feel like the first chair flute player in his orchestra, but he never gives me the music so I can perform at my best or deliver what he wants.

"I'm a Christian woman, and I know God doesn't like divorce, but now that the children are gone, I live in a constant state of fear and anxiety. I can't sleep. I'm exhausted trying to figure out what's going to happen next. Years ago, he moved his teen children into our home one at a time without any discussion or notice they were coming. By then, we had two small children of our own. I felt stuck in a kind of insanity that no one even suspected from outside. We looked like the successful, all-American family."

I felt certain I could help Ella reclaim her life and take back her personal power to make better choices for herself. She had clearly lost this ability during years of constant conflict, verbal shaming, and the discounting of her personal and professional contributions to their blended family. Richard now treated Ella as if she didn't exist in the house. She felt insignificant, invisible, and out of control of her own emotions. Richard used "stone-walling," like the "silent treatment," when he wanted to avoid any decision-making or discussion while cutting off communication for days.

"Richard rarely takes responsibility for anything that happens," Ella told me. "He usually twists around what I say until it becomes all my fault, as well as my responsibility if I want anything changed."

Ella was puzzled about Richard's behavior, and I was curious about his childhood and recent past. Richard had retired from a long and successful professional career. He was aging, and health issues made it difficult for him to regularly play his favorite sport. He was anxious and agitated most of the time now, and he regularly told Ella she was the one who was angry all the time.

I inquired what Ella knew about the kind of family Richard grew up in. He was the oldest child of five. His father worked by day but tended bar nightly while drinking regularly as Richard was growing up. Because of his father's neglect, Ella's future husband had become his mother's surrogate spouse and confidant, helping her with everything she needed. She was always complaining about how nothing her husband ever did was good enough, so she would burst into tears, relying on Richard to comfort her.

Richard resented not having the nice things his peers had and felt awkward—like he stood out in a crowd because he didn't have nice clothes or live in a nice house. He never believed he could attract the popular, good-looking girls, and he secretly hated the other boys, whom he viewed as having better luck than he had. But since Richard was the only child to attend college, his mother was proud of him and focused on his achievements.

Ella said Richard always commented first about every woman's appearance. It started with his mother. He was embarrassed by her appearance because she never looked as good as the other moms did. Richard's father was so passive and absent from his daily life that he always longed for that male approval while never feeling that he got it.

Richard's mother manipulated him into taking care of all her "illnesses." Ella believed his mother was a true hypochondriac—never happy or satisfied, yet controlling everyone around her with her sicknesses and victim mentality.

Richard's mother also confided in him behind his father's back, telling Richard his dad wasn't much of a husband. Raised by a narcissistic, controlling mother with a passive, absent father left Richard vulnerable and lacking the skills to even know how to have a healthy marital relationship.

He picked Ella for her attractive, well-groomed appearance; she was a college graduate several times over. However, it was obvious that Richard lacked the ability to trust women for fear of being engulfed by another one, so he worked to develop an exterior of excellence while concealing his internal lack of self-worth. He never felt good enough, comparing himself to all his peers while concealing the inner rage he had stuffed for a lifetime. Richard prided himself on not getting angry. Instead, he buried it deeply ... until Ella said or did anything contrary to his expectations.

Ella was Richard's third wife. Sadly, he couldn't understand why his first two wives both had extra-marital affairs. It was obvious from Ella's story that Richard was totally closed off from his own wounded, emotional self, which was the result of having been used as his mother's narcissistic supply.

Richard had been neglected and abandoned emotionally by both of his parents. As a result, he couldn't relate to or really feel comfortable with any woman. After all, the first woman in his life—his mother—used him to meet her own self-centered emotional needs. This set him up for failure in his adult relationships because children or teens can't meet the emotional needs of a parent, nor can they take on the emotional responsibilities of a father who neglects his own marriage.

Richard continued that same behavior in each of his three marriages by emotionally neglecting his spouses. He was angered each time Ella expressed her needs. Particularly when physical illness incapacitated her, Richard neglected and abandoned Ella physically, leaving her to fend for herself. There can be no intimacy with a heart closed off by years of having to consider another's needs first. Richard had no idea how to relate to an adult woman unless he was in charge and the boss. When Ella tried to express her own thoughts, feelings, and ideas, Richard took it as a personal affront, believing one more time that he couldn't do anything right or even "good enough." Thus, he often accused her of "attacking" him.

## Janet's Story

Let's now turn to Janet's story, which involves a lifetime relationship with a mother who is both narcissistic and alcoholic. You might want to consider any similarities in actions or words from Ella's story—or from your personal experience. Twenty years before, Janet had been part of a codependency group in my office where she'd disclosed growing up with an abusive, alcoholic mother. For the past eighteen years, Janet had overseen her mother's life, health, and the troubles she regularly got herself into.

Janet's mother was clearly narcissistic from an early age. She was adopted into a family when her mother died early in her life and her father couldn't raise her alone. Her mother was viewed as very special in her adoptive family where she was doted on like a princess because she was loved so much.

But Janet's mother had no tolerance for her own children and seemed void of any motherly instinct. Despite having a twin sister and a younger brother, Janet and her siblings barely had food for school lunches. Their mother spent most of her time sewing pretty party dresses for herself. Janet took over her mother's household and child-care responsibilities at an early age, saying "when life got too hard, Mother just checked out and was taken to the local hospital to dry out for a few days."

Janet now needed help dealing with her eighty-four-year-old mother's out-of-control behavior that regularly involved calling the police to assist in getting her to the hospital emergency room for treatment. By now, Janet's mother had been diagnosed with bipolar disorder, but she rarely took her medication. Always combative, taking no responsibility for anything that happened to her, Mother continued to wield violent threats and abusive words at Janet. Janet was simply trying to move her to a safe environment. Her mother believed she was just trying to lock her up somewhere.

Janet was at the end of her rope. She tearfully described the guilt she was feeling at the thought of having to secure guardianship over her mother. Yet Janet was keenly aware of her mother's manipulative ways and lying behaviors that she had always used to get what she wanted.

By the time I saw Janet, her own health was seriously deteriorating as she expressed concerns related to obesity, pending diabetes, depression, and anxiety to the point of occasional panic attacks. Her sleep was seriously interrupted, and she'd been taking sleep medications for too long.

Janet finally confessed to me, "I've been drinking one or two glasses of wine nightly to calm my nerves so I can sleep and be ready to return to a stressful job the next day. When I have to be around my mother, it feels like something sucks the life right out of me. I feel so much guilt. Although I keep praying about what to do, I finally decided I can't handle this alone."

Despite her mother's obvious lifetime issues with alcoholism and bipolar disorder, Janet was not yet aware of the level of Narcissistic Personality Disorder that was present in her mother's words, actions, and general ways of thinking. These had not changed since Janet was a young girl. But now, at the age of eighty-four, her mother was alone, lonely, and frightened—but still defensive about letting others get too close to her. Her alcoholism had hardened her, and her heart had always been closed to anyone except herself—all characteristics of NPD.

Let's think about Janet's story for a moment. Can you see that her mother's adoptive parents were so glad to have her that they elevated her sense of self-importance way too high? She became entitled as a result, placing her own importance well above the safety of her own children. Janet's mother never had to be responsible for anything growing up since her parents covered for her mistakes. Her inflated sense of self-importance caused her to abandon her own children emotionally and physically. Like a child trapped in an adult body, Mother couldn't recognize her own children's needs. You'll come to understand a little later how Janet became codependent, constantly doing for Mother—now to the point of exhaustion.

There are countless other examples that define the narcissist's true nature.

Consider the boss who gives by taking: "I'd like you to run this big meeting for me. It will give you a chance to show off everything I've taught you."

Think about the so-called close friend who excuses herself with a dig disguised as an apology: "Sorry for being so late to meet you, but I know your schedule is much freer than mine, and I guessed you wouldn't be doing anything important this afternoon anyway."

Or the jealous sibling who unloads a stinging remark that bursts your bubble when you get a promotion: "You'll have to get your kids new cell phones so they can remember who you are."

And the spouse who chooses to parade some of your faults in front of friends, only to openly chide you for being too sensitive, followed up with this comment: "Honey, can't you ever take a joke?"

Or the example of the older adult son who has squandered his own financial resources and now comes crawling back to an aging mother, looking for a handout. As the mother provides a guest house rent free in exchange for getting her to doctor visits, he voices to an older sibling who now manages Mother's finances that he believes he should be paid mileage in spite of the fact that he's using the family car for his personal use.

I truly believe that no one asks for a life filled with the things we've just heard—the attitudes, the ways of reacting and responding to others, having to carry around hidden rage over things that happened to us as children over which we had no control. It's important to remember that the person who turns into a narcissist may have had no more choice in his own early development than we initially did about picking these types of personalities to form a relationship with. Had we known what would happen, I doubt any of us would have chosen this for those with NPD ... or for ourselves. For these reasons and others, it's important to consider increasing our empathy and compassion for those affected by this damaging merry-go-round of highs and lows on both sides of this disorder—for the perpetrator and for the victim-survivor.

"The extreme stress and trauma that most often occur as a result of narcissistic abuse can make the victim appear crazy," writes Shannon Thomas, LCSW-S, in her blog post "Healing from Hidden Abuse, A Journey Through the Stages of Recovery from Psychological Abuse." "Crazy" in these cases describes the victim's mental confusion, emotional reactiveness, defensive responses, memory impairment, and likely sleep deprivation from chronic adrenaline output.

Consider that chronically being around these individuals with the kinds of "toxic" behaviors demonstrated can literally make you sick. The behavior of the narcissist defies logic, and a normal person becomes more and more incredulous and defiant in their response to the narcissist's behavior over time. The narcissist uses the other person's reaction to their abuse to convince them that *they* are in fact the disturbed and unstable one, the one who indeed needs help, which is a form of "gaslighting" behavior. What the

NPD person advocates to everyone who will listen is that he is truly the victim. He will use the victim's response to his insidious abuse against them as a means of justifying to others his own victimization.[2]

These same types of behaviors are being demonstrated more and more in today's corporate arena where pressures to succeed are paramount—intense competition occurs within teams; bosses, managers, and coworkers use bullying and other noxious behaviors to manipulate others; and those same people can be found barking orders while making snide remarks behind backs to derail and undermine someone else's success to get ahead.

"Toxic behavior," says Georgetown University's Christine Porath, Ph.D., "doesn't just inflict personal hurt, it assaults systemic well-being, while generating stress and frustration through the constant and crippling devaluations of another individual."[3]

We call it *relational trauma* when one person betrays, abandons, or refuses in some way to provide support for another with whom he or she has developed an attachment bond. These situations constitute attachment injuries, a rupture in the relationship bond. Researchers are now describing a phenomenon in which the betrayed person is so overwhelmed by their own inability to find the capacity to cope that they now struggle to define the very nature of the original relationship. This destabilization re-defines what was once a safe haven in times of stress as a source of immense and imminent danger.[4]

Whether in your primary relationship, your family, or your workplace, being around this toxic behavior can literally make you sick. The destabilizing impact of these kinds of treatments are reported to be linked to cardiovascular disease, insomnia, depressed immunity, and compulsive overeating—to name only a few.

Post-Traumatic Stress Disorder (PTSD) is often the result as victims try to respond, either by attempting to reconnect with the perpetrator or by building walls around themselves to prevent more damage to their hearts because of painful rejections and lack of care demonstrated by someone who is supposed to care and love them. PTSD manifests in many and various ways. When repeated and intermittent woundings occur, regardless of the type, the abused partner is highly likely to begin to show signs of PTSD. When the abuser is a narcissist, this same phenomenon may be referred to as Narcissistic Victim Syndrome. Though not complete, a listing of PTSD symptoms includes ...

- Increased feelings of anxiety among relationship partners
- Hyper-vigilance—scanning the environment for potential signs of threat or danger
- Paranoia and overwhelming terror at times, including agoraphobia
- Insomnia
- Exaggerated startle reflex
- Avoiding reminders or conversations, as well as not remembering all aspects of interactions (called blocking)
- Re-experiencing events through thoughts, nightmares, memories, flashbacks

- Increasing distress over time that impacts all life areas to include self-care, work, daily responsibilities, along with the ability to participate in other relationships[5]

Psychological trauma usually follows and accompanies relational trauma events such as sexual abuse, rape, domestic violence, ongoing emotional and verbal abuse, long-term extreme poverty, and sexual betrayal. We are discovering from psychological research that when these traumatic events happened during the formative years of a narcissist's life, he resorted to drastic defense measures to deal with the internal pain, shame, anger, and rage he was experiencing, yet had no way to express. When people live with this kind of trauma, they experience shock to the core of their being and no longer feel safe in the world. Without any lifeline to hold onto, the victim experiences hopelessness and despair. Symptoms of depression and anxiety can overshadow the motivation to live and thrive. Victims of more severe trauma mentioned above may additionally experience the following symptoms of PTSD:[6]

- Hyper-arousal, helplessness, sleeplessness, immobility, anxiety
- Reliving the event, hyper-vigilance, nightmares, intrusive images
- Withdrawal, avoidance, mood swings, panic attacks, phobias
- Flashbacks, denial, oversensitivity, depression, restlessness

- Confusion, dissociation, inability to eat, overeating, rage
- Health problems (auto-immune, endocrine system) and Chronic Fatigue

Being part of a relationship with a narcissistic person on any level can ultimately result in personal relational trauma, regardless of the specific type of relationship, whether boss/employee, parent/child, sibling/sibling, friend/friend, or primary love relationship. The methods of betrayal are all manipulative means the narcissist utilizes to control, seduce, overpower, and exploit others to meet his own narcissistic needs. The consequences to others are of little concern for the NPD person. His primary goal is to prevent any cracks in his cover-up, though he may be totally unaware this is the force driving his actions.

The mental health community has for years primarily focused upon the needs of the abuser since alcoholism, drug addiction, sex addiction, compulsive gambling, and other addictive behaviors are often involved. Twelve-Step Groups provided a source of support for these individuals as well as for the partners who were abused. Al-Anon, Nar-Anon (Narcotics Anonymous), Codependency Anonymous, or Co-Sex Addiction Meetings were often found to be places of hope where injured people could share their stories of intense emotional pain. Narcissistic abuse with its toxic behaviors is reported to have increased in the past ten years, while victim-survivors are finding they need much more help than was formerly recognized.

Family of origin dynamics often provide "the grist for the emotional dependency mill" in our lives. Individuals having grown up in families affected by poverty, alcoholism, drug addiction, crime, and major health issues are often prime targets for the charismatic, extroverted, energetic, hard-working personas often presented by the grandiose narcissists. Emotionally dependent people find themselves attracted to what seems familiar, even if the other person presents differently at first. Enabling, detachment, and effective boundary setting are skills required to help partners heal. These will be discussed later in this text.

More clients are experiencing all types of sexual betrayal in their relationships in general, often due to the availability of Internet services. However, sexual infidelity is clearly a part of the grandiose narcissist's behavior as well. Regardless of the form of sexual betrayal, from pornography to forced sexual participation, we now know that "those persons who were betrayed and violated by sex addicts were searching for what they could no longer find: safety in unsafe relationships. The result is that victims are left broken and separated from the very people with whom they felt their deepest attachment bonds."[7]

A vital part of healing for survivors of incredible relational and often sexual trauma requires that empathy be mirrored back to them along with a level of deep understanding. They need to feel validated and affirmed as people of great worth and value. Offering hope for the restoration of their own lives is imperative. The pain they have endured at the hands of those who they most loved, trusted, had built a life with, and possibly had children with is often found to be incredibly shocking, gut-wrenching, and impossible to understand—even more so than any sudden death of someone close, or even a serious medical diagnosis for themselves.

The "heart of the matter ... is the matter of the heart." Their hearts have been ravaged, broken, and torn apart.

Dr. Barbara Steffen, trauma researcher and psychotherapist, reports that "in one moment of life, security is replaced with betrayal and the death of lifelong dreams. Such a discovery causes adrenal glands to dump cortisol into the body's system, triggering the 'fight/flight/freeze' response to danger. She now knows the inherent danger of loving a compulsive liar, the person with whom she lives, sleeps, and invests time and feelings in, participates in hidden (sexual) behaviors that jeopardize finances, personal safety, health, and even her life, not to mention the lives of their children."[8]

These actions are referenced to those people identified as sex-addicted, although the description is no less meaningful for the survivors of narcissistic abuse where sexual infidelity is also extensive. Very often, living in relationship with a narcissist feels as though a victim's life energy is literally being sucked out of them—and they don't know how to plug the drain. Communication is difficult—even impossible at times—preventing resolution or agreement. Family members and friends become resentful, depressed, anxious, and even hopeless at times when the narcissist dominates every gathering. Or he may act in a covert way, hanging back, wanting others to notice there's something wrong.

But the narcissist seems incapable of sharing in an honest, open way with anyone—unless it's about what someone did to him. Victims often find themselves asking, "What happened to the person I first met, befriended, or even married? Where did they go? What do I need to do to get that person back and get back to that place?" Let me begin with an important story that I think may serve to demonstrate some of the deepest roots of NPD.

## Tapping the Root of Narcissistic Personality Disorder

We are all aware of the existence of narcissism in our lives as we listen nightly to the news of the horrors happening to people in every city, town, and neighborhood. We may not have known what to call it, but narcissism covers the gamut from incredible rudeness to complete lack of respect. The "me first" entitlement attitude is seemingly found everywhere we go.

Terrorist activity carried out by those who believe they are superior demonstrates their belief in their ability to decide who lives and who dies. A narcissist believes in this kind of control—undergirded by fear, buried rage, pride, and shame—but often without guilt, remorse, the ability to take responsibility for their actions, or the ability to feel empathy or compassion for the pain they inflict upon others. Do we fully understand the cost to the people touched by narcissism? How can we possibly measure the impact this disorder has upon the life of the person who has a narcissistic personality? He didn't ask to have this affliction any more than the diabetic asks to become diabetic!

When God opened my eyes to the emotionally abusive environment of my own long-term marriage, I slowly saw the many destructive ways I'd fought back against the abuse. I had no idea I was dealing with a disorder that had changed the husband I loved from the inside out. I saw how I had enabled the very behaviors I loathed and railed against, "unfortunately using only the weapons of the world." The more I learned about this affliction and the ways I'd tried to defeat it, I believe God brought more women— and a few men—into my own counseling practice, the TapRoot Centre, for healing. They, not unlike the runaway slaves that were part of the underground railroad system in southern Ohio, found their way to this historical site built upon hallowed ground, once believed to be a "safe-haven for the slaves on their flight to freedom!" (circa 1893). Those victim-survivors of narcissistic abuse have also been captives, not unlike the slaves bound by some force that seemed to have no name yet caused them to "run for their lives." These are the people who I have spent time working with intensely over the past many years of my career.

Living with or being in the company of a narcissist may feel like a kind of slavery or captivity as our own desires, wants, and needs are sublimated to the control of the narcissist. Never could I have imagined God would help me come to know the enormity of this hidden problem in today's culture through the personal adversity I experienced in my own marriage. Clearly, I was not alone in my plight. Many like me were living as captives to something we couldn't see or understand.

People who knew us didn't want to hear our personal stories of intense pain, the kind that left us feeling crazy, even though we felt desperate to be heard and understood. It appears no one could identify with us when we talked about the behavior changes happening in the people we loved. The people who knew the narcissist in their professions, workplaces, at church, or in casual social situations couldn't grasp that what we described and experienced was abuse. What was most confusing is that even as I sought to be heard, I continued for a time to help my husband, a narcissist, look good to the outside world—like a perfect couple who had it all together.

Feeling insignificant, isolated, and often invisible, victim-survivors in narcissistic relationships need a safe place to talk about what we've lost and how we've come to feel about ourselves. Telling our stories without fear of blame, judgment, criticism, or shame is about disclosing the truth and unspeakable pain, loneliness, and isolation of living in the shadows of a narcissistic individual—too often behind closed doors.

## The Earliest Beginnings of a Narcissistic Personality

The greatest story of all time began in the Garden of Eden when our enemy, Satan, manipulated the fall of all mankind. Before the first bite of the forbidden fruit was eaten, God foreknew that we would sin by our willful disobedience. And God already had a plan for the redemption of His people before Adam and Eve sinned. Satan was enraged that he was hurled out of the Garden because of his own willful disobedience. Satan's power-hungry, arrogant, pride-filled attitude was intolerable to an all-loving God, so he was banished from heaven forever.

History then is "His Story," God's story of the Fall of Man. Satan, filled with pride, envy, and jealousy, became our adversary. His ways were seductive, cunning, and designed to create doubt in Eve's mind about what God had said, who God really was, and whether He might be holding out on them.

When Adam and Eve chose to listen to the seductive voice of the enemy, they lost their innocence. Instead, they acquired the knowledge of good and evil. They realized they were naked. They felt afraid and exposed. They became vulnerable to sin. Their attempt to cover their nakedness was a symbolic gesture of attempting to hide the truth of their disobedience and their vulnerability to sin from God—and possibly from themselves.

Our relationship with an all-loving God was broken in the Garden of Eden, and now sin is part of all humanity. When we disobey God, we really know at some level what is right and good and what is wrong and harmful. When we feel bad about what we've done, we feel guilty. When we feel bad about *who* we are, our shame breeds fear, anxiety, and the drive to hide our very selves.

As if the royal couple—Adam and Eve—was being chased by a tiger, their thoughts now turned toward what God would think of them. "What if God really sees who we are and what we've done? Surely, we'll be banished from His sight." Although they were guilty of sinning, the greater truth was that humanity was now plagued by the characteristics that Satan alone possessed—pride, arrogance, self-centeredness, selfishness, desire for control, wanting what he wanted, and more. Can you see now how Satan was the "original narcissist"—the O.N.—of all time?

When each of us realizes our own vulnerability, we often experience both fear and shame, now part of our human condition. Shame is the powerful emotion that causes us to feel less than we are—not good enough. Its painful sting leaves us all desperate to avoid ever feeling it again. So, through the process of projection and blaming, just as the O.N. did to Eve, someone else is left to carry the pain for the narcissist—the victim in the relationship.

Refusing to take responsibility for their own words and actions, the narcissist piles it on us so that we feel their shame and we experience their pride—the opposite of shame. Consider when Joe the jokester tells a coarse joke in mixed company and no one laughs. Generally, Joe then picks a target and inappropriately makes fun of that person so that instead of recognizing the narcissist's faults, he manipulates others into laughing along with him. Afterward, we feel guilty for participating.

If you're the target, you should know that the shame heaped on you by the narcissist doesn't belong to you. They make you believe the shame is yours. If you have no ability to say otherwise, if you feel you have no voice to stand up to your accuser, you now feel worse while like Joe, he's left feeling better about himself. This is not unlike how Satan operated in the Garden, and it is much the same way narcissistic people operate to cause others pain.

Narcissists often appear to be "puffed up" and high minded, expressing that they know better than anyone else. The root word in Greek is *tupho* and has the meaning of making smoke. Like a smokescreen, Satan has blinded the eyes of prideful unbelievers so they are unable to see the truth. From the same root comes *tuphoo*, meaning high minded, proud, or inflated with self-conceit.[9] Not unlike Satan the O.N., the narcissist possesses many of these same character qualities and more.

Suppose the personal characteristics of deception, doubt, fear, shame, and blame are foundational components of the narcissistic personality. It's possible that what has been overlooked is the idea that pride blinds a person from being able to discern the truth. Without a scientific way to research this premise, aren't we all capable at times of experiencing some of these same emotions within our hearts? When we do, we try to hide who we really are, masquerading as someone we are not.

Satan harbored deep resentment against God and anyone who was close to God. He was and still is power-hungry, caring little for the harm he causes to achieve his own personal goals. These are the primary weapons of the enemy, and as we will see, many of these same traits are sadly characteristics of the narcissist.

Another story from Greek literature tells of young Narcissus, a handsome young fellow who appeared in Greek mythology. We are told that he was proud of his indifference and disdain toward the nymph Echo as she relentlessly tried to pursue him with her love. However, the gods ultimately punished him by cursing him for his unkind, negligent responses. As a result, Narcissus fell in love with his own reflection when he could not pull himself away from gazing daily at himself in the pool. He became so enraptured with his own beauty that the tale ends when Narcissus finally wastes away, dying alone as he could neither eat nor drink because of his need to secure attention and affection from the only one he could not possibly secure it from: himself. A flower called the narcissus, commonly known as the daffodil, was named in his honor.

Narcissism may in fact be an outgrowth of the seed of deception, lying, shame, and blame sown in the Garden that fateful day. After that, we became a broken people before we were ever born. God's plan to restore humanity to his heart included Jesus Christ coming to earth as a sinless man to die on the cross, taking on a substitutionary role on our behalf, as the only way to free us from our sin. We all sin and deserve to be punished. But God offers us His gifts of grace and mercy, the forgiveness of our sin, and redemption through our faith in the work of Jesus Christ on the cross.

So what is different in the life and innermost being of a person who believes he must remain in control of his own life? Narcissists proclaim they don't really need anyone, yet they use other people in harmful ways to meet their personal needs. However, to those whose faith has carried them this far, we contend the narcissist needs our empathy, compassion, love, and hope for a better future for them and for those around them.

As many of you have experienced, though, this can be quite a challenge. Depending upon the specifics of your relationship, it may seem difficult if not impossible to even consider empathizing with the narcissist, especially if you are still in the company of the NPD person. Before we move on, let's consider the words offered by Sarah Young in *Jesus Today*: "I am your risen Savior! Through my resurrection, you have been born again to an ever-living hope. It is vital for you to remain hopeful, no matter what is going on in your life … When storms break upon your life, you can find only one adequate source of help—Me!"[10]

# CHAPTER 2

# Nothing Is Wasted, Especially Your Suffering

No one who hopes in you will ever be put to shame.

—Psalm 25:3a[1]

Jenna came to my office with complaints of chronic depression while revealing she was using alcohol daily to help her relax. She was still a young mother and felt ashamed that she was doing this. She was adamant that she feared turning out like her own mother from whom she'd been estranged for years. I asked her to tell me a little something about her past relationship with her mother. Her face darkened, she looked away, and she began to cry, hiding her face in shame.

Jenna's mother was a classic narcissist. Having grown up in a poor, Irish-Catholic family in New York, her father was a violent alcoholic who regularly beat her mother and older sister in front of her. She would escape to the little neighborhood church where she could sing and where she learned to play piano. Her rich imagination allowed her to survive her brutal home life by fantasizing herself as "daddy's little princess," a star of the stage and a great concert pianist—a role she kept hidden from family while living out a lie.

Jenna described her mother as selfish and self-centered, thinking only of herself even when there was no food in the house and only inadequate clothing for her five children. Jenna was terribly confused by this as a young girl because she knew her father was a successful businessman. Jenna quickly became her mother's secret keeper, believing this would bring her special attention from Mother. But by the age of twelve, she discovered that her mother not only had a lover but that she also betrayed all her children when the truth was finally exposed much later that Mother was not a great concert pianist nor a star of the stage.

Jenna's mother led the family to believe her hours away from home were spent perfecting her craft. One can only imagine the shock and feelings of betrayal felt by her husband and children when they later discovered she had a Romanian lover, an immigrant who worked as her accompanist at the little church she attended. Mother demanded Jenna's time as a way of comforting herself while she exposed shameful stories of her escapades—too sensuous for Jenna's young ears to ever have heard.

Her mother also repeatedly verbally bashed her father, complaining that he controlled her with his money, when in truth she was exploiting him to pay off her lover. As if that weren't damaging enough, Mother told Jenna that her father was unfaithful, too, because that's just what adults do. Jenna felt sick at the thought that her family would be destroyed if she revealed the truth, which became imprinted on her heart, feeling the shame of her mother's actions every day of her young life.

By age fifteen, when Jenna began acting out by smoking marijuana, drinking, experimenting with drugs, and coming in at all hours of the night, no one was there to care or set boundaries for her. She felt burdened and ashamed and didn't want to hear her mother's grand tales anymore about her heartsick lover. Jenna's mother behaved shamelessly, parading naked through the house singing just because she could. Despite her brothers' pleading with their mother to stop, she continued as she pleased as if they weren't even there. Mother projected her shame onto Jenna by never taking ownership of the manipulative lying and deceitful stories she manufactured. And when Jenna tried to confront the woman with the truth, her narcissistic mother would lose control of herself and rage at her, saying, "What a stupid little fool you are! You're only a child. You don't know anything."

By the time Jenna walked into my office, the stronghold that was preventing her from getting her own life back was found in the words, "You stupid little fool! You don't know anything!" Her mother squandered her own life. Jenna's father eventually divorced his wife, and her children and grandchildren could no longer trust her, so they set wide boundaries between them. However, Jenna was left with a belief that she wasn't good enough to do anything right. After all, she couldn't fix her mother. Her parents' marriage ended anyway.

Jenna's heart began to soften over time "by the grace she experienced in her personal relationship with Jesus Christ." She remained separated from her mother for years due to the emotional strain and trauma that resurfaced from being around her. Jenna could never trust whatever her mother told her. Judas's betrayal of Jesus is a characteristic pattern for the narcissist who always believes his way is best—even when the consequences are grave.

Jenna knew that Jesus would forgive her mother and change her mind and heart, if only she would turn toward Him and ask to be saved. That had not yet happened. Jenna learned that loving her mother didn't mean she couldn't make her own choices to care for herself. She recognized her mother had nothing to give her. God changed Jenna's heart so she could see the tragedy of a life gone wrong. She has great hope that one day she will be able, by God's grace, to minister to her mother by sharing the truth of the gospel message. Forgiveness and compassion for her mother's narcissistic affliction are rising in Jenna's heart, but only by the grace of God.

As difficult as Jenna's story is to hear, imagine a mother who would exploit her entire family for personal gain! I shared this story with you so you might understand that in a family where abuse is occurring, even if it doesn't happen to you, it results in a need to survive by whatever means possible—in this case, Mother took on a mask, a covering for the great pain, shame, and guilt she experienced when exposed to the beatings her mother and sister endured. Her sexual encounters were her only attempt to find love and acceptance as she had no ability to be intimate with anyone. She had shut down her emotional self as a child in order to survive the intense pain and humiliation—sadly something that was re-created in her own life.

The prevalence of NPD has been estimated to be 6.2 percent of the population in the United States, with higher percentages of

7.7 percent for men, followed by 4.8 percent for women. Those numbers approximate that 20 million people could be directly afflicted with this narcissistic disorder. It's impossible to calculate the number of others who are deeply affected, even traumatized, by the repeated verbal, emotional, and mental assaults for which they require psychological and psychiatric help to heal.

Harvard Medical School researchers have also reported that NPD rarely manifests alone, so family and friends are affected as well when the NPD person potentially has a host of co-existing conditions. They report an 11.9 percent incidence of mood disorders to include major depressive disorder; 11.5 percent incidence of anxiety disorder; 8.8 percent incidence of substance use disorders, as well as sexual addiction, alcoholism, and eating disorders, to name a few.

Although little research has been done regarding any biologic factors that may contribute to the development of NPD, Harvard Medical School researchers also offer lifetime incidence statistics to include the additional co-morbid conditions that often exist with NPD. Additionally, 23.8 percent of narcissists develop bipolar disorder; 19.9 percent develop panic disorder and agoraphobia; and 22 percent suffer from drug dependence, particularly with alcohol and cocaine.[2] Recently, eating disorders have been added to the list of co-occurring conditions. It seems clear from these revealing statistics that NPD is associated with considerable disability, especially for men whose rates exceed the incidence in women.[3]

Researchers have been plowing through an immense amount of data during the past ten years trying to piece together what's happening in the culture and what societal changes have helped to create this emotional burden in the lives of so many. What is obviously true is that narcissism is on the rise. In Dr. Craig Malkin's book *Rethinking Narcissism*, Dr. Malkin shows why he believes that we all possess a bit of narcissism. A Harvard Medical School psychologist and lecturer, he believes this describes the part of each of us that fuels our self-confidence and allows us to take risks such as seeking a new job or asking a new person out on a date. When the characteristic manifests in a way that the person thinks himself too special, perfect, or better than others, this becomes a problem for the individual and for those around him.[4]

A research group from San Diego State University has identified a higher incidence of narcissism in younger generations. Although the Narcissistic Personality Inventory (NPI) has been highly critiqued, stating it contains only desirable traits, the authors strongly support its non-biased nature by demonstrating the inclusion of statements like "I can live my own life any way I like" and "I find it easy to manipulate others" as evidence of a more than balanced view.[5]

"Narcissism seems to be a widely growing social disease with no end in sight!"[6] Some would say that narcissism is the dark side of individualism, represented by "freedom without responsibility, relationships without personal sacrifice, and positive self-views with limited grounding in reality."[7] Several important factors, which we will discuss in more detail later, have played an important role in the development of this social disorder: parenting styles of younger generations; the celebrity culture; media and the Internet; and finally, the availability of easy credit, allowing people to think they are wealthier and more successful than may be the truth.

Researcher Dr. Jean Twenge also cites the 6.2 percent lifetime incidence of narcissism.[8] In analyzing years of research from baby boomers to millennials, Dr. Twenge highly supports the growth of the "me-first" mentality. Reports indicate that millennials tend to play more games in relationships and lash out more frequently when they are criticized or feel challenged in any way. The foundational structure of their lives may be represented by vanity, material possessions, and fame.

## Relationships with People Who Have NPD

You might be asking by now, "What does all this mean for those of us in relationship with an NPD person?" One researcher describes these relationships this way: "Disordered people aren't just hurtful, they are capable of spinning our reality to make theirs less painful. They project their problems onto us, and blame us for what they do. After a time of living in the company of the personality disordered, it becomes difficult to distinguish what is real from what is being projected and what is being distorted. We begin to doubt our reality and question whether we are the crazy ones—if we haven't already been told by the narcissist, 'You are crazy.' More importantly, disordered people hide their problems very effectively, while concealing their disease from most others, causing others even further confusion. The truth is—they are not right! They feel better when they can get us to carry the burden of their illness and their behavior."[9]

Family therapist and clinical psychologist Joseph Burgo, Ph.D., talks about the fact that what we initially believe about the narcissist is that they only love themselves because of what we see them clamoring to achieve and demonstrate outwardly. He believes this is a behavior, a defensive posture developed to keep at bay the painful internal feelings they may experience or experienced at an earlier time in their lives. They have developed a powerful delusional system of thinking to avoid the painful truth of how they really feel. If we express interest in them, this fuels their interest and desire, and they are adept at being able to arouse the same in us.[10]

The narcissist's goal is to identify a "supply" of others who can and will continue to provide them with the affirmation, affection, and the attention they seek. Sadly, this often happens at the expense of the person doing the giving. This is a part of the defensive external mask or imposter self the narcissist wears to avoid having to feel the pain, shame, and fear of vulnerability that is deeply buried inside him. As we consider how narcissists fuel their supply, it may be cause to pause here to ask these important questions: "Just who are the people who are attracted to narcissists, and what is it about these people that draws the narcissist to them?" Let's take a closer look.

Let's talk for a bit about what it's like to live with and/or be in relationship with a narcissist. Have you noticed that your wants, needs, desires, and life goals take a back seat to his expressed interests? He is looking for a partner to complete himself. His supply resembles someone who is attracted to him and lets him know it. They may be highly impressed by what the narcissist knows, so they respect him and look up to him. Because his need for affirmation is constant, he needs those pats on the back—about everything. He generally wants someone who matches his style and taste so he looks good in public, so he searches for a partner who also takes pride in her own appearance. He needs someone who demonstrates she is capable of handling responsibility while demonstrating her own personal talents. In short, he's in search of a person who mirrors all of who he believes himself to be. He sees himself as fiercely independent, yet he wants the ability to control the person he attaches to. This individual is generally emotionally dependent and, through her own early wounding, has developed extensive codependent behaviors while having lost her own ability to feel or focus on what she needs or to have a voice.

Remember Ella? She came from an alcoholic family with a father who was narcissistic and controlling. His method of controlling his children was to instill fear in them by telling them things like, "No matter where you are or what you're doing, I will know!" She lost her voice at an early age and tried her best to be perfect—just the sort of person Richard was looking for. You may be wondering whether the narcissist consciously takes control of emotionally dependent others. I cannot answer that specifically; but I do believe he looks for those who he believes can be controlled so the chance for his own vulnerability to be exposed is lessened.

Family systems where alcoholism, substance dependence, mental illness, medical illnesses, or other major problems are present make it nearly impossible to think independently, express ideas and have them validated, or express feelings openly without repercussions. It is likely that emotionally dependent people are familiar with the chaotic, confusing, rules-always-changing kind of environment in which alliances are severed or not allowed and promises are meant to be broken.

Shame is passed around like candy at Halloween, and "walking on eggshells" becomes not only the feeling experienced in the external environment, it also sets up the trauma reaction of "fight, flight, or freeze" in the internal environment of every person who lives in the family. Being part of a narcissistic relationship can very quickly feel familiar, almost comfortable. Care-taking behaviors with weak boundary-setting skills are just what the narcissist is looking for. This allows the narcissist to take control, focus on his needs alone, almost without even having to ask. It's truly hard to even conceive that he wouldn't realize that others have needs, too.

Any kind of intimacy with a narcissist is relatively impossible since his emotional life seems buried so deeply that he has disconnected from his own feelings. Although most researchers believe them to be quite vulnerable, demonstrated by the ease with which they can be triggered into a narcissistic rage, the extent of vulnerability they seem so desperately trying to hide is not exactly known. In the early stages of a relationship, they appear to be able to feign intimacy by watching other people or their partners and mirroring their actions and words.

Have you noticed that over time you might have lost touch with your own feelings because you've become so fixated upon the needs and wants of the narcissist in your midst? Have you become aware that some things about you have changed since he may want you to dress a certain way, act differently somehow, do certain things you are uncomfortable doing, or participate in particularly degrading sexual acts? Have you found that over time your self-esteem and self-respect have eroded until you find yourself neglecting your own physical, emotional, and spiritual needs? The mounting stress can result in physical illness, which may include gastrointestinal problems, ulcers, high blood pressure, cancers, depression and anxiety, and eating disorders. In advanced stages, there have been reports of suicide or premature death in partners.

On an emotional level, partners, family, and friends experience feelings of alienation, isolation, and intense bitterness. The following list identifies clusters of cruel behaviors, indifferent attitudes, and difficult or uncontrollable circumstances that people have reported when dealing with the NPD person:

1. Feeling drained of all energy and personal resources (emotional, mental, financial).

2. Plummeting self-worth while questioning your own sanity.

3. Conditional strings keep you as part of his "supply" while he claims his generosity.

4. You come away feeling ashamed for asking to have your needs met. Your needs will always take a back seat to his.

5. You feel isolated when the NPD wants to interfere or make attempts to consume your time, attention, and whereabouts.

6. Jealousy is expressed for the time you spend with family, friends, and colleagues while you question whether the jealousy is sincere since becoming more available to him does not increase his interest in you.

7. Expect the use of sarcastic, sadistic humor at times, including threats to your safety, as in, "When I'm done with you, I'll just throw you in the lake."

8. Any attempt to compromise will leave you feeling like you're the only one who gave anything.

9. Expect conversations to become heated arguments so that he can lash out at you.

10. Beating him at his own game is not possible. He is highly competitive and when cornered on some truth or feeling challenged in any way, he will rage, make rash decisions, even demonstrate erratic thinking.

11. Expect to be made to feel responsible for nearly all decisions, often followed by being told how controlling you are.

12. Although the primary problem lies with his NPD, expect yourself to be focused on his co-occurring disorders, while you encourage him to seek help for his addictive behaviors like compulsive spending, gambling, alcohol or drug abuse, or sexual addictions and infidelity. The incidence of ADHD is also reported to be higher than in the general population for NPDs.

13. Spending time alone as they age or retire causes them to become more negative, complaining about people who were once friends.

14. Recall that they have no empathy, so do not expect compassion and caring when you are

injured, sick, or hurt. Their primary concern in getting you well is so you can return to fueling their supply.

15. When you ask them to stop bothersome or harmful behaviors, don't be surprised if they don't listen to you. Some researchers believe they are at least intellectually aware of the hurtful things they do to others. However, the reason they refuse to stop is simple—they don't care what you want.[11]

16. As an emotionally dependent person, you often become more caring and kind in the face of ongoing mistreatment. Recall your attempts to be kinder and more helpful. Has it predicted ongoing frustration, hurt, resentment, and feelings of betrayal all over again as you continue to enable him? If you do not first establish healthy boundaries, you may be opening yourself to more abuse.[12]

17. As a victim-survivor, the repeated experience of the kinds of behaviors reported here will most often result in significant emotional and psychological trauma. These behavioral patterns are abusive, neglectful, and dangerous. A more complete listing of the behaviors employed by narcissists is included in the Appendix.

If you still have questions, the following vignette will demonstrate how real these behaviors can be. I imagine if you're living with an NPD, you have already experienced some of these yourself. I don't mean to be preaching to the choir, but it's still important to be reminded that these are damaging behaviors, and even though they are not about you, they can be traumatizing.

Joan heads a team that together has been very successful in increasing sales by sixty-four percent over the past two-year period. Overnight, Joan's female boss began to challenge every detail of her work. Joan reported heightened anxiety, second guessing everything she did. Just minutes before the start of an important executive team meeting, Joan's boss demanded she put together a proposal highlighting the team's success. Fully aware of the limited time frame, along with the fact that her team and all the corporate executives would be present, Joan attempted to meet the challenge. From the moment the meeting began, Joan realized she'd been set up by her boss—scapegoated to bear the brunt of public humiliation at the hand of her incompetent supervisor before the whole executive team. Joan soon realized her boss was unprepared to speak about her own team's success. Joan came to counseling to learn how to establish appropriate boundaries for herself as well as her coworkers, who also had been subjected to vicious attacks.

G.I. upset, headaches, loss of appetite, increased anxiety, and difficulty sleeping over the past several months were all symptoms Joan reported. She and the entire department walked on eggshells daily. Even the assistant department head was not willing to confront this barracuda after having been shamed publicly for responsibilities that were clearly not his. Joan began to realize that today's public shaming was not much different from every previous incident in which someone's head went rolling—especially when the boss feared "she" might look bad to the higher-ups. She would spare no expense to humiliate someone else to save face for herself.

## Signs of Relationship Trauma and Abuse with NPDs

- **Physical signs:** headaches, sleep disturbances, gastrointestinal upset, ulcers, rashes, tension, muscle spasms, generalized body pain, racing or irregular heartbeat, appetite changes, and some cancers reported.

- **Emotional symptoms:** fearful, depression, anxiety-ridden, withdrawal and complete disconnect from others, mistrust, hyper-vigilance, crying, numbing emotions, toxic shame, unrelenting guilt, inability to focus or concentrate, memory difficulties, chronic confusion, or feeling crazy, excessive irritability, and increasingly eroding self-worth to name a few.

- **Spiritual signs:** include feeling convicted or confused, keep the truth hidden, withdraw from time spent with the Lord, doubting what you truly believe.

- **Mental signs:** obsessively thinking about the person and his behavior, at times excusing or minimizing his actions in your mind and to others, chronic worry, and overly focused on all relationship aspects with NPD person.

Those living and working in close relationships with narcissists report additional relationship experiences that "they put you down so they can feel elevated themselves."[13] Here are some examples of what that might look and feel like:

- You avoid communicating with them as you feel put down, confused, discounted, and emptied of all you know.
- When you approach them with any personal need, you come away recognizing your needs just took a back seat to theirs, while you feel ashamed for even having inquired.
- Should you ever receive an ingenuous apology or compliment, expect to leave feeling patronized, demeaned, and even humiliated.
- Attempts to compromise end by your recognizing that you were the only one who gave anything.
- Looking for affirmations for hard work and a job well done is only acknowledged in the service of helping meet his selfish demands. Otherwise, you might expect to feel used, abused, and for the truth of your interactions to be distorted.
- They use a sarcastic, sadistic humor at times, making threats to their partner's safety, i.e., "When I'm finished with you, I'll just throw you in the lake."

In general, people who live with or work closely with narcissistic people describe how their own personal feelings of self-esteem and self-worth are slowly eroded. We will begin to understand more as we consider some potential causes of the NPD disorder in the next chapter. We may better understand then how the people who view their behavior report it to be very childish. Like people who refuse to grow up, when trials and conflicts arise, they are reported to revert to outbursts that may appear tantrum-like. And finally, when they feel backed into a corner, they may come out acting like a victim, even saying things like, "I know, I know, it's all my fault!" with a significantly sarcastic tone and an attitude of insincerity that is palpable.

The dependent partner, coworker, friend, or family member most often feels used, cheated, betrayed, and taken advantage of. Promises are never kept, opportunities described never materialize, shared dreams for the kind of life hoped for blow away like smoke.

## Emotional Bonding through Trauma

"The key to understanding behavior found in abusive relationships is to look at the very early years of childhood. Relational trauma is at the root ... There are several features these kinds of relationships have in common. The first is, they are deeply ambivalent, reflective of the Trauma Bond—fear, dependency, need, fear of abandonment, despair, the realization of helplessness, and rage. This is an amalgam of powerful emotions that drive and make the relationship so unstable ... The second feature of this kind of relationship is that it is a compulsive reenactment."[14]

Although anyone can experience an abusive response to the narcissist's behavior, those who have previously experienced any form of abuse or neglect earlier in life may be more susceptible to being re-traumatized in these relationships, while forming an invisible bond via the trauma itself.

God created our brains to help us survive since He knew that life would be hard. During trauma, powerful chemicals bathe the body to prepare the victim for fight, flight, or freeze mode, commonly known as a trauma response. Some of these are stress hormones like cortisol. But additional chemicals are also released during intermittent episodes of abuse and neglect. "When the person uses excitement, fear, sexual aggression, extreme behaviors, and risky situations to force us to cling and bond, this is reactive living and the victim does not have a conscious choice."[15]

These chemicals automatically activate an internal biochemical bonding process, much the same way a mother bonds with her newborn child. Bonding with a marital partner during sexual intimacy results in a positive loving experience that brings the couple together intimately. However, when a woman is repeatedly traumatized (regardless of the approach used) and it occurs intermittently, a trauma bond results. This supports the difficulty victims experience when trying to escape their harmful circumstances. The emotional pain she experiences, fueled by fear, shame, and guilt, results in a withdrawal process that now occurs because of having lived in a chronic state of readiness fueled by adrenaline.

Because male biochemistry is dramatically different and males do not possess the same hormones, it's reported to be easier for males to cut ties and move on in search of a new narcissistic supply. The Stockholm Syndrome is the name given to the process whereby the victim bonds to the abuser for survival purposes. This generally happens only in the most toxic cases of NPD and other kinds of violent abuse.

Although what you have just reviewed might be disturbing, it is imperative you maintain hope that change is possible. Both you and the narcissist in your life are victims of problems he doesn't even know exist, despite your repeated attempts at telling him how hurt, unimportant, and beaten down you feel. You have done the best you possibly could do with what you knew at the time. Take heart! You need a different set of skills to deal with the narcissist in your life. And that is exactly what I hope to be offering you here. I encourage you to keep reading!

# CHAPTER 3

# A Darkened Mind

For this people's heart has become calloused; they hardly hear
with their ears, and they have closed their eyes. Otherwise
they might see with their eyes, hear with their ears, understand with their hearts and turn, and I would heal them.

—Matthew 13:15[1]

Tori and Kevin came in for a session because the tension between
them could be cut with a knife—if they didn't cut each other first.
Kevin was an airline pilot … a captain. Flying is, was, and always
would be the "love of his life."

Tori was as mad as a roused-up hornet's nest. She quickly
spoke up in an angry yet loud and tearful tone so no one could
mistake what she was saying. "We're here because Kevin tells me
that if I don't do something about this weight, he'll never have sex
with me again!" Tears streamed down her face as she sputtered
out how Kevin was unfaithful to her almost as soon as they got
married. "I loved him. And it's the only reason I've stayed. From
the start," Tori said, "our marriage has never been his top priority."

Kevin grew up in the hills of Kentucky with a daddy who was
angry, mean, and alcoholic. When his daddy went on a bender, he
knew to stay out of his father's way. Kevin remembers those beatings with a belt—pants down, spread eagle, and anyone within

earshot knew that Kevin had screwed up again—or maybe not. It seemed that Kevin could never get the approval that he longed for from his father. Like all of us, we ache at times just to hear the words, "Good job, Son. I'm proud of you!" But Kevin never got that—at least not from his daddy. He'd already decided to become a pilot, so he worked hard to make top-notch grades in high school.

Kevin's momma coddled him, trying to make up for his father's failures as a parent, but Kevin never gave up trying to please his daddy. He became momma's helper, a role that required him to stuff his anger and rage for having to do what was his daddy's job. He later felt justified in unleashing all that shame and rage he'd stuffed away because of all the things he missed growing up. Early in life, Kevin began to use women for sex, feeling good about the control he finally had. A narcissistic attitude had been modeled by his father, even the carousing with women. A kind of competitiveness that can be enormously damaging developed. The more Kevin progressed in his studies and personal achievements, the angrier and uglier his father became toward him. Kevin could do nothing right.

Kevin's behavior didn't change just because he married Tori. Make no mistake, Kevin declared that he loved his wife—his extramarital affairs were just part of his extracurricular activities. Kevin believed that "What Tori didn't know wouldn't hurt her." The flying job that kept Kevin at home was suddenly eliminated, so he told Tori that to support all *her* spending habits, he'd have to sign on with a foreign airline. It would take him away from home twenty-one days every month for the next five years.

Tori felt left behind—abandoned without any voice in the matter—to raise their three teenage children. Abandonment was one of her greatest fears, a deep wound from her own abusive childhood.

While Tori poured out her heart, Kevin leaned back in the chair, all six foot, four inches of him, with a smirk on his face. Kevin finally spoke up, saying, "I've been telling her she needs to do something about that weight she's carrying. I know she comes from an abusive past with a stepfather who was a dry-drunk and the pastor of her church, but she needs to put that past in the past and get over it," Kevin said. "I read my Bible every day," he added, exhibiting the kind of arrogance that sends chills up your spine. "That's how I deal with pain and disappointment."

Tori chimed in, "And you use it to tell the rest of us how wrong we are about everything—especially how we spend *your* money!"

Is it any surprise that you might identify Kevin as a narcissist? From the start, what Kevin wanted from Tori was what he got—without discussion. Kevin's early infidelity was fostered by those well-intentioned others in his life who had already been wounded themselves and probably adopted the idea that giving too much praise spoils a child. Mother's efforts to make up for Daddy's lack may have done more harm than good. She created a dependency in him that he hated. She controlled him. As an adult, he would take control in every situation he could.

Controlling others became the name of his game, no matter what he had to do to achieve it. Sadly, Kevin's father is *still* a toxic, alcoholic narcissist. But the one thing Kevin seemed to need the most was his father's approval and admiration. He was still trying to please his father and now risked losing his wife of thirty years and connection with his own children.

At this point, you might be asking why siblings who grew up in the same family affected by wounded parents didn't all become narcissistic. Let's take a closer look at how the narcissist learned to protect and defend himself from the painful emotional assaults he experienced during his formative years.

## Developmental Thoughts about Our Inner Imposter

Let's begin to turn our thoughts toward a more complete understanding of the underlying foundation for the development of NPD. We'll begin as a point of clarification with a few words to remind us of the impact of the Fall of Man in the Garden of Eden and man's separation from our Creator, leaving us to live our lives apart from God. Next, we will take a look at the development of what's commonly called the inner imposter, a concept coming out of addiction research which describes how, in our brokenness, many of us feel such shame and humiliation about who we are that we fear being exposed and known by anyone. This aligns with what we see in the NPD's behavior: the need for a cover-up. These findings will be highlighted with words from author, speaker, and psychotherapist John Bradshaw—pioneer in the Adult Children of Alcoholics era in the late 1970s and into 1980s.

What we'll be proposing in more depth is the idea that the child who becomes narcissistic may have been born with these human tendencies, and then his life experiences may have also threatened and traumatized him in a manner that caused him to seek ways to cover up who he believes himself to be—or who others have told him he is. We will then break down some of the so-called types of narcissists; however, we will remember that the basic character components regardless of descriptor remain the same. And finally, we will end this segment by highlighting a few of the well-known people who clearly demonstrate narcissistic presentations across the NPD continuum. Take a deep breath to get ready to go—and let's begin together.

When God created each of us, He knew we would all be flawed. But still He created us in love and prepared the way for us to grow toward the goal of perfection, which is impossible to achieve until eternity. God sees our real selves with all our imperfections, flaws, sinfulness, and doubts. The "Good News" is that He accepts us as we are—flawed and imperfect—and loves us just the same.

God also knew that our families would have parents and care-takers who were also flawed. Attachment ruptures have occurred to many children in broken families, leaving them without the security, safety, and the ability to connect with trustworthy others. When it's time to launch, they are unprepared for adult relationships. Like children and adolescents in adult bodies, their interactions and reactions are immature, and attaining any kind of intimacy is nearly impossible.

John Bradshaw, in *On the Family*, one of his most notable works, states that "we learned to survive by sacrificing ourselves. The roles we took on, not chosen by the individual but rather assigned by the needs of the family system, occurred as a means of trying to get our needs met. The roles set us up to behave in ways that were not who we were authentically created to become.

We learned to attempt to control other's behaviors and actions by becoming heroes, caretakers, scapegoats, lost children, the responsible one, surrogate spouses, our parent's parent, the rebel, the problem along with other patterns of behavior."[2]

To survive, we became dependent on behaviors that we learned to act out, trying to get our needs met. We abandoned ourselves emotionally by denying the truth of what we saw, not acknowledging the truth of what we knew to be true, and not expressing feelings of our own.[3] Potentially, this laid the groundwork for a disordered way of functioning in the world and possibly for the development of NPD.

We neglected our very selves in the hope of salvaging our lives and our families. What we learned to do was to neglect ourselves to survive the emotional pain of being shamed, finding ourselves alone, and experiencing a kind of self-rupture that left us feeling powerless and spiritually bankrupt. To survive and remain safe, the abandoned child self now takes on a false or imposter self—not really who he is.

The child self needs to idealize his caretakers to hold onto the hope for survival, and so he must make himself—rather than his wounded caretakers—bad, unworthy, undeserving, and less than who he is. Because he now feels so bad about himself, he projects onto others these forbidden parts of himself, while internalizing his parents' or caretakers' voices. What this means for the child self, and later for the adult, is that every time he experiences a personal need, feeling, desire, or a want that was shamed or rejected as a child or teen, he continually re-experiences the same shaming voices internally with the same kind of dialogue he experienced as a child. "Shame is no longer only a feeling—it has now become an entire identity. The authentic self has now withdrawn itself from any *conscious awareness* within the individual."[4]

The narcissist is terrified of his own shadow self—the long-hidden child who may have been irreparably damaged and whose feelings of inadequacy drive him to overcompensate and compete with a vengeance. Looking within and risking any level of self-reflection is to be avoided at all costs because, for the NPD person, it represents the unbearable vulnerability he has avoided all his life. This also supports the fact that narcissists rarely seek therapy, avoid honest communication, refuse to be accountable for anything, and readily resort to defensive raging behaviors and outbursts to try to blunt the truth.

Therefore, when this occurs in an individual's life, the makings for a very narcissistic self will soon develop and emerge from the attachment ruptures of unmet childhood dependency needs. This view also supports what others who are not threatened by the NPD's actions report to be almost childlike.

What this inevitably points out is that the child-self had no real say in what happened to him. In his innate need to survive, he responded by disconnecting from his own self to take on a disguise that would allow him to survive and hope to get along in the world. If this process took place early enough in his life, the potential for him *to even be aware* that this occurred is very small. Is it any wonder then that he believes there is nothing wrong with him? The behaviors he demonstrates become all that he knows of himself. His inner spiral of inadequacy drives him toward survival—because nothing else really matters. Since we know that our human condition is one of poverty (of spirit) and woundedness, this is what we tend to reject about ourselves, and in place of self-acceptance of our humanness as wounded people, the "seeds of a corrosive self-hatred have taken root."[5]

This self-hatred, fueled by life experiences that support his belief, and a lack of acceptance by the individual, could potentially form the personality that expresses narcissistic behavior, revealing itself by adolescence and early adulthood.

When someone has been traumatized repeatedly by the painful experience of being shamed or publicly humiliated—like being bullied—the individual comes away being told or even believing that he is less than a human being. When this happens, the self in all of us retreats to a safer place inside where no one can reach us. Only a few of the defenses he develops to protect himself from threat include denial, dissociation, repression, withdrawal (flight reaction), anger, identification with the persecutor, and re-enacting behaviors.

The impact of these kinds of stressors is great, and depending upon how long an individual must endure them, these patterns become a way of life, no longer experienced as survival skills. The degree of the stress can range from mild, resulting in chronic fear, to severe traumatic events that leave lasting imprints in the human psyche. While these behaviors were at one time protective, they have now become destructive for the individual. It is speculated that these imprints are stored in the subconscious mind where the brain operates automatically to assign meaning while creating emotion and sensations to correspond. This then becomes a part of the reactionary response system and re-enactment pattern also seen in Post-Traumatic Stress Disorder (PTSD).[6] What we are describing here can be foundational to the development of NPD as well as several other types of disordered personalities.

If the individual with narcissistic personality disorder has been repeatedly traumatized throughout his formative years, it is conceivable that the character changes reported in the body of psychiatric literature make the simple diagnosis of any personality disorder more complex. Judith Lewis Herman, M.D., reports, "All too commonly, chronically traumatized people suffer in silence; but if they complain at all, their complaints are not well understood."[7] Attempts may be made repeatedly to treat their symptoms while the deep underlying issues of trauma go unaddressed.

Dr. Herman goes on further to report that, "In survivors of prolonged, repeated trauma, the symptom picture is far more complex. Survivors of prolonged trauma develop characteristic personality changes, including deformations of both relatedness and identity."[8] Both these qualities are uniquely characteristic of NPD. Dr. Herman previously proposed name changes in the American Psychiatric Association's Diagnostic and Statistical Manual (DSM-IV) that these cases be called Complex Post-Traumatic Stress Disorder. Other psychiatric researchers also have made references to the personality changes that follow prolonged and repeated trauma exposures.

The heading "Complex Post-Traumatic Stress Disorder" includes individuals subjected to surviving domestic battering, childhood physical and sexual abuse, and other types of trauma. Of interest is the fact that under this proposed descriptor, symptoms that could be characteristic of NPD include many of the following:[9]

- explosive or extremely inhibited anger (which may alternate)
- compulsive or extremely inhibited sexuality (which may alternate)
- alterations in consciousness that may include both de-personalization and de-realization
- alterations in self-perception, including shame, guilt, and self-blame
- sense of complete difference from others (which may include a sense of specialness, utter aloneness, or a belief that no other person could understand)
- alterations in relations with others, including isolation and withdrawal, disruption in intimate relations, persistent distrust
- alterations in systems of meaning to include loss of sustaining faith

Although this is only a speculative assumption based upon research of victims who have survived both major catastrophic trauma as well as childhood trauma, I believe it is not unreasonable to consider that the individual who feels the need to protect himself in the world from the potential exposure to any form of re-traumatization and its effects could potentially be changed and develop one of several named personality disorders to include NPD.

This in and of itself compels us to consider having significantly increased empathy, compassion, and love for the abused, neglected, betrayed, or abandoned inner child self. The narcissist has never had the opportunity to heal a wound so profound that it has forever changed who he is or who he was meant to become. If the narcissist in your life, regardless of the relationship you may have now or have had in the past, was a child standing before you— could you truthfully say that you could feel toward him anything less than great empathy, compassion, and love? Imagine, too, that for him to survive his own circumstances, he unknowingly took on a cover that forever changed the way he views people, relationships, community, the world, and God. Can you only imagine?

Consider the case of a thirty-five-year-old woman who came to see me with an eating disorder that began around the age of twelve. When asked what it was like to grow up in her family, her head dropped, and tears began to fall. She was the only girl with five older brothers, all of whom bullied and teased her incessantly. She was fearful, withdrawn, and described that in addition to her eating disorder, she also was being treated for fibromyalgia, an auto-immune disorder.

She described her personal experience at the family dinner table this way: "When food was set on the table, all five brothers and father filled their plates to the full, while my mother and I shared what remained, which most often was very little."

No boundaries were set, no respect shown, and no one intervened when my client was the brunt of coarse jokes at the table. Without any boundaries, the boys teased their sister about her developing body, particularly focusing on her breasts. In her humiliation, she realized then that women were not to be valued—in fact, they didn't even deserve to eat. Although she became a para-professional in the healthcare industry, now in her mid-thirties, she remained unmarried and had a significant fear of men. She purposely made herself quite unattractive. That coupled with her anorexic frame, now devoid of any breast development at all, enabled her to feel somewhat hidden and safe from being approached by men. Anorexics have a deluded belief that the thinner they get, the less others will see them—notice them, yes—but really see who they are? No!

In this case, the narcissistic father taught his sons to have no respect for women. Even though my client and her mother did all the work in the home, the men all came to the table feeling entitled not only to food first, but to belittle and shame their sister, possibly to avoid becoming the target of their father's narcissistic wrath. The seeds of narcissism were sown by example and demonstrated through the woundedness of the father who came from a rigid German heritage where abuse and narcissistic behavior were commonly acted out.

The imposter self now an integral part of the person's identity behaving in a manner not unlike one who is bound, chained, and held captive is described more clearly in this way: "Like runaway slaves, we either flee our own reality, or we manufacture a false self that we hope will be more lovable, more acceptable than the true self we believe is neither."[10] We believe this to be the plight of the narcissistic self.

This false self or "imposter" self is the beginning of a disease process that is now rooted in the fear of human disapproval. The imposter self now becomes preoccupied with a strong focus on achievement, acceptance, and approval, along with a suffocating need to please others. Rarely can the narcissist risk letting this guard down for fear someone might see or know his truth—that he is flawed—while the excruciating feeling of shame and vulnerability is triggered repeatedly. Remember, because this is an external image, the narcissist seems not to feel compelled to maintain this cover at home, and so his closest "supply" often suffers in silence, just as he did as a child.

The glamour of the false-self blinds the narcissist to the truth of the depth of his own emptiness. To fulfill their emptiness, they may develop a compulsive need to fill up with food, gamble away their hard-earned resources for the challenge of gaining more, or step outside committed relationships and marriages for just one more attempt at feeling desired or wanted.

Craving what his painful wounds have stolen from him, he enters each day with an insatiable appetite for more—like looking one more time in the mirror, hoping not to see what he fears most ... his real self. His narcissism causes him to be preoccupied with whatever he believes will shine a better light on the external facade he has created. We will see this more clearly as we describe the various categories of narcissistic behavior. These imposter selves, remember, have been created so that no one will really see and know how truly unacceptable he feels as a human being.

The imposter self cannot experience intimacy in relationships because he lacks the ability to feel compassion and empathy. His narcissism excludes others in judgmental assessments of their abilities and of their character. Incapable of intimacy with his own self and out of touch with his own feelings and intuitions, he craves more and more. Driven by his inherent need to survive, his tactics become ever more deceptive and damaging as his fear of being exposed is heightened.

We're reminded in Scripture that "our love of money is the root of all evil, and some by longing for it, have wandered away from the truth and buried themselves with many griefs."[11] Consumption has kept people spending, designing, investing in more to the point that we have lost our connection to the values and purpose upon which we are building our lives. Life has become independent of any philosophy or creed upon which it was first based. We consume out of our personal desire for more without motivation—while the center of our lives remains empty and void. This identifies much about the way the narcissist operates in life. Everything outside of him that he believes reflects a favorable light on him and him alone is worth pursuing.

Sadly, when anyone disconnects from their spiritual center and becomes intensely focused on trying to maintain an exterior image of success, it leaves no opportunity for real relationships with others. Does this help you gain some understanding of the depth of the emptiness, the loneliness, and the intense fear of being vulnerable the narcissist experiences daily?

Over the past several generations, parenting styles have resulted in many "child-centered" households where parents tell their kids "they are the best" without demonstrating commensurate perfor-mance. Not only can this result in setting unrealistic expectations for kids, but telling kids "you are special to me" may be far better than telling them "you are special." A simple "I love you just as you are," rather than helping them think they are better than others, goes a long way to helping kids connect with others vs. feeling as though they must stand above.

Family expectations, along with praise and affirmation for accomplishments not truly deserved, can alter the development of a child or adolescent's self-esteem while impacting the child in many other ways.

## The Many Disguises of Narcissism

Before we move into identification of several categories of narcissistic behavior, let me mention how it is that this might be important to include. Remember that narcissism falls on a continuum from traits and features to full-blown clinically diagnosable NPD. Becoming aware that various behavioral patterns seem to exist may help you clarify what you may be dealing with and personally experiencing. Let's begin with just a brief review of a few generalities about the disorder.

Narcissism belongs to a category of afflictions that we call personality disorders. All personality disorders fall on a sliding scale of severity. In general, they all describe the disability in terms of a person's inability to manage their emotions; hold onto a stable sense of self and identity; and possess a pervasive inability to maintain healthy relationships at work, at home, in friendships, and in love. And these characteristics are enduring over time.[12]

According to several narcissism researchers, for any individual to be diagnosed as having Narcissistic Personality Disorder (NPD), the individual's ability to function must manifest on the extreme end of the continuum, affecting and impairing daily functioning in the areas of identity, self-direction, and conflict due to their lack of empathy and intimacy in most—if not all—relationships.

Key researcher Craig Malkin, Ph.D., has more recently posed the concept of a fluctuating empathy vs. a complete lack of empathy as had been first considered. NPD people are indeed able to feign empathy by observing and emulating true examples of empathy seen in others. But their behavior often creates such antagonism and/or attention-seeking that it becomes pathological on many levels.[13] Attempts at communication with them often leaves others frustrated and confused.

Research has indicated a high correlation between child abuse and the development of Personality Disorders (PD)—73 percent involving abuse and 82 percent neglect. A group of personality disorders in which narcissism falls reports more types of trauma exposure and higher rates of physical abuse.[14] The DSM-IV manual also reports that those individuals who experienced more adverse psychosocial experiences in childhood might clearly support the development of an adult personality disorder (PD). Cluster B group includes the following PDs: Antisocial, Borderline, Histrionic, and Narcissistic.

The fact that the terms narcissism, narcissist, and NPD are often used interchangeably makes it difficult for researchers to get an accurate picture of what people are truly experiencing. Many factors are directly and indirectly responsible for the development of NPD, although it seems the most prevalent causes seem to be related to attachment breaks or ruptures during one's formative years, basic genetic makeup that is part of the spiritual wounding from the Fall of Man, relational and emotional injuries during the socialization process that include examples like bullying and shunning, and the cultural messages and lifestyle of the times in which we live. Regardless of the combination of factors involved, this malady expresses itself across a continuum of behaviors, thoughts, and actions.[15]

Lundy Bancroft, another noted researcher and psychotherapist, confirms that an abuser's behavior is based in his psychological and emotional injuries in addition to his relational deficits.[16] Bancroft also supports and believes this behavior springs from his early cultural training, the key role models in his life, peer influences, neighborhood, TV exposure, the books he reads, and the jokes he's heard. His abuse of others is a result of the values he's developed. When his attitudes and beliefs are challenged, the NPD tends to reveal a contemptuous and insulting personality that normally stays hidden, reserved only for private attacks on his partner. He tries to keep friends, relatives, and therapists focused on what he feels (remembering what we've just learned about his disconnection to his emotional self) so that his real thoughts will not be revealed—perhaps because at some level he knows the true nature of his problem—*out of the heart, the mouth speaks.*[17]

Here is a recap of many of the characteristics that move a person toward a clinical diagnosis of NPD and toward the extreme manifestation of the disorder, remembering that these fall on a continuum of characteristics displayed as traits and features, whether manifesting overtly or covertly.[18] As you review this list, try to put yourself in the place of the narcissist as a child or adolescent who may also have been neglected, abandoned, abused, used, and bullied. Many of the behaviors acted out upon innocent others may be a re-enactment of what he first experienced and is ferociously trying to never experience again:

- An obvious self-focus in interpersonal exchanges
- Problems in sustaining satisfying relationships
- A lack of psychological awareness and insight
- Difficulty with empathy or a total lack of empathy
- Problems distinguishing oneself from others (evidenced by no boundaries)
- Hypersensitivity to real or imagined insults (often resulting in narcissistic rage/injury)
- Vulnerability to shame rather than guilt
- Haughty body language
- Flattery toward people who admire and affirm them (narcissistic supply)
- Detesting those who do not admire them (narcissist abuse)
- Using other people without considering their wants, needs, or desires
- Seeing themselves to be more important than they are
- Bragging (subtly but persistently) while exaggerating their achievements
- Claiming to be an expert in many things without compensatory evidence
- Inability to view the world from the perspective of other people
- Denial of both remorse and gratitude

## Grandiose Presentation of NPD

Let's begin with a discussion of the most well-known form of narcissism. The more grandiose narcissist is the one most people think of when they hear the word *narcissist*. You know, the person who knows everything about everything while having no difficulty presenting himself as an expert—whether this is the truth or not.

The more grandiose narcissists, who seem to range on the high end of the narcissism scale, also seem to experience higher highs and lower lows. If the world is not verifying their greatness, they might react by becoming depressed. When life stresses such as job losses, divorces, a failed business plan, or disappointment of some nature occur, they respond in a way that indicates a bruised and dented self-image and ego. They may become intensely defensive, spewing their anger and rage. When the admiration and praise they believe they deserve, often without commensurate achievements, is not forthcoming, the narcissist might lash out, aggressively attacking others in turn for the perceived assaults they believe are being inflicted upon them. In short, they are hypersensitive to any criticism.

When loss occurs, they may react by believing it to be a real attack upon them, as if they have been singled out on purpose. Their vulnerability, which they believe themselves to be immune to, is challenged, and their moods, behaviors, words, and actions all reveal their intense shame and vulnerability—all symptomatic of an unhealed internal wound.

## Covert Presentation of NPD

The less well-known category of narcissism is found in the individual who most would never suspect of being narcissistic at all. That's why today's researchers have identified more than one type of narcissism based upon the way the disorder manifests in word, action, emotions, and attitudes. The vulnerable or covert narcissist tends to be introverted while expressing a far more sensitive temperament. Their grandiosity is hidden because of their introversion with a tendency toward shyness. They fantasize about their greatness more than advertising it. At times, they don't appear to fit any definition of narcissism. They're not into socializing, not intent on drawing attention to themselves, and in general, they appear quite laid-back. Their introversion drives them into deeper silence and, at times, into intense misery to cling to their feelings of specialness. They might imagine themselves as just doing it differently, being the most misunderstood person in the room, an undiscovered genius, or a long-suffering martyr.

Even when they are shy, they have a way of sucking all the air out of the room. Some researchers believe a better descriptor would be "introverted narcissist." However, they are anything but hidden or invisible. This individual, although shy, is described as having a deflated sense of self-worth, inadequate self-perception, and much greater awareness of one's own internal emptiness. He lives with unfulfilled expectations as it seems he creates grandiose fantasies in which he is at the center of his own world. He seeks constant approval from others and is like the Borderline personality in his need to please others. It has been identified that he carries a chronic internal resentment as he sees others having and experiencing most often what he wants yet cannot get.

The more covert narcissist surrounds himself with others he sees as inferior while secretly envying those who possess a high level of accomplishments. Although making great efforts to keep himself out of the limelight for fear of public humiliation or rejection by others, he has a marked propensity for feeling ashamed. Because he is unable to depend upon or trust others, he generally focuses upon his children as a means of securing the power and glory he is in search of. He possesses an intense inability to see his own partner as a separate person with one's own interests, rights, values, thoughts, and attitudes.[19]

## "True Colors" in the Face of Conflict

All narcissists reflect their true colors in the light of conflict. If we consider the fact that the narcissist is an emotionally wounded person, we can begin to conceptualize more clearly the idea that he exhibits behaviors that help him disguise or assuage the pain of his wounded inner self. For all of us, when conflict arises, even the healthiest of us become defensive and self-protective.

Unlike normal people, though, when the NPD experiences real or perceived conflict, they are unpleasant to be around due to their argumentativeness and arrogance. It is when they are under pressure that they fully expose their lack of empathy, the true cornerstone of a narcissist. A question has been raised about their ability to be vulnerable. Two current researchers both take the position that the narcissist is, in fact, an emotionally wounded person. The behaviors he exhibits are efforts to disguise or assuage the pain of his unhealed emotional wounds. The inability to ask for assistance or to risk vulnerability indicates the depth of his own fear and insecurity.

## The Most Damaging Behaviors of the Narcissist

The most toxic of NPD behaviors seem to follow a pattern of abuse. The narcissist requires a narcissistic supply—an individual or a group of people who fulfill their demands for attention, which often results in isolation and separation from their own sources of personal support for those who comply. The behaviors they adopt are most often hurtful, verbally abusive, involve acts of betrayal, offer no options for conflict resolution, and can involve physical violence and sexual abuse.

It is possible that the behaviors a narcissist displays might be an indication of the extent of harm done to their developing self-image during their formative years. The way they act out as an adult may mirror very closely what they experienced as a child.

Below is a list of the types of interactions most often occurring in relationship with an extreme or pathological narcissist:[20]

- Ignoring requests to cease behavior that is hurtful to another, such as lying, cheating, and stealing.
- Name-calling, criticizing, belittling, mean jokes, verbal jabs made publicly.
- Serial infidelity (use of pornography, social media, prostitutes, etc.).

- Repeated arguments over the same issues, without resolution, particularly when one person is being hurt or harmed in some way.
- Turning conversations around in a way that the partner's expressed concerns are used to blame them and block ongoing conversation.
- Partners are constantly frustrated because they do not feel heard, listened to, or understood.
- No closure, apologies, accountability, consequences, or charges for damaging actions.
- Partners suffer the consequences of the narcissist's repeated patterns of destructive behavior and choices (alcohol and substance abuse, sex addiction).
- A general attitude of not caring exists. The narcissist rarely experiences remorse for inflicting physical or psychological pain on others.
- To maintain power and control over others and their environment, they use their power to subtly put others down. Previous world leaders known for using this approach include Hitler, Muammar Gaddafi, and Saddam Hussein.

## Additional Faces of Narcissism

Many narcissistic people have made significant contributions to the world in the fields of medicine, politics, music, the arts, and sciences. Many are great philanthropists as well. Those of us on the outside admire them. But sometimes we hear about breaks in their facades—abusive and broken marriages, multiple kinds of abuse, criminality, and even murder. Let's take a brief look at various situations that may give rise to narcissism, recalling that NPD exists on a sliding scale of severity.

**Acquired Situational Narcissist**—develops in late adolescence and is generally brought on by wealth, fame, or characteristics of celebrity status. The individual comes to believe they are more important than other people. They often believe in their invulnerability—as might be characteristic of Justin Bieber. Bieber is often in the news as he seems to live on the wild side, always calling attention to himself, regardless of what he is involved in. It might be said that he seems to attempt to operate above the law!

**Sexual Narcissism**—is defined by an inflated sense of sexual ability and entitlement. It involves the erotic preoccupation of themselves as a superb lover with the desire to merge with one's mirror image. It is identified as a dysfunction disorder in which sexual exploits are pursued, generally in the form of extramarital affairs, as a way of compensating for their low self-esteem and inability to experience true intimacy. Some researchers might liken this to what we commonly identify as sexual addiction.

**Spiritual Narcissism**—describes a person who uses the Gospel to build themselves up while tearing others down. They constantly reference their own spiritually based achievements such as their latest published book, Bible series, or ministry development. They memorize Scripture to support their own agenda. They are quick to speak and slow to listen when others need to express their needs. Jim Jones could be considered a well-known spiritual narcissist who managed to set himself up as a kind of spiritual god. People who more easily needed someone or something to follow to direct their lives were used and abused, ultimately sacrificing their lives. Other examples also exist in the Christian world—some in our own hometown churches.

**Celebrity Narcissists—Making the Celebrity 100 List.** The world's highest-paid celebrities pulled in 5.1 billion pretax dollars over the past twelve months according to *Forbes Magazine*'s Top 100 Celebrity List. Singer/songwriter Taylor Swift tops the list with earnings of 170 million dollars. At twenty-eight years old, Swift leads the list of highest paid female celebrities within the past six years. But that doesn't mean she is a narcissist. It only indicates that she could be. It's often difficult to penetrate beyond the public persona of a celebrity. Although situational narcissism may be what we are describing, this in no way diminishes their talent, hard work, and creative ability.

Other celebrities who fall into this category include Kim Kardashian, who posted 365 photos of herself on Facebook assuming that the world thinks so highly of her and her life that everyone in the world would want access to her, not just her husband for whom she first took the photos as a birthday gift. Lady Gaga, with her song lyrics "I live for the applause," is often seen in outrageous costumes and makeup that seem to call much attention to herself. Although a talented artist, her singing alone would garner attention. Although there are many celebrity artists who may or may not be viewed as narcissistic, Madonna has admitted during interviews for TV's *20/20* that she was often claiming with her attention-seeking costumes and presentations, "Look at me!" How could we possibly look away?[21]

Dangerous but well-known people with NPD include power- and control-hungry narcissistic men such as Adolf Hitler, Joseph Stalin, O. J. Simpson, and Ted Bundy the serial killer. They all exhibited irrational thinking, a sadistic exploitation of people, and demands beyond human understanding of their need for control, all carried out without guilt or remorse.

There is some evidence to support a genetic predisposition to NPD. It's generally accepted that narcissism develops early in life as a defense mechanism that helps the individual deal with emotionally painful situations. If narcissism is a learned behavior, then there may be some hope that the behaviors and attitudes can be unlearned with appropriate targeted interventions along with a range of treatment options. But people with narcissistic personalities are stubborn, inflexible, and not prone to admit their problems or the need for help.

Yet narcissists are often lonely, have superficial relationships, possess an extreme fear of failure, and suffer with significant anxiety. Only at the point in their lives that relationships or employment have been significantly impacted might they consider some form of treatment. Those NPDs on the extreme end of the continuum are often poor candidates for therapeutic change. But those who display a significant number of annoying, hurtful, or damaging traits related to their interpersonal interactions may find their way into treatment because of a despairing spouse's urgency or through threats of divorce.

Researchers believe that some narcissistic people can grow beyond their condition. Their damaging behaviors were and possibly always have been a serious attempt to survive minute by minute.

If we believe that their behaviors, attitudes, and ways of relating in the world were modeled for them when they were children, then perhaps it is possible they can unlearn those negative traits. We can hold onto our hope and have compassion for them as we begin to explore treatment options and suggested interventions.

# CHAPTER 4

# Treatment Interventions for NPD

Some became fools through their rebellious ways and suffered afflictions because of their iniquities. They loathed all food and drew near the gates of death. Then they cried to the LORD in their trouble, and he saved them from their distress. He sent out his word and healed them; he rescued them from the grave.

—Psalm 107:17–20[1]

Research continues to improve treatment for all mental and emotional disorders. The recently released DSM-V, commonly known as the Diagnostic and Statistical Manual of the American Psychiatric Association, has determined that narcissistic traits, features, and characteristics are commonly found in the group of personality disorders called Cluster B—antisocial, histrionic, borderline, and narcissistic.[2]

One common characteristic of people with these disorders is their insistence that they are special and privileged. When individuals think they are so different and unique that no one would be able to understand or relate to them, this is called *terminal uniqueness.* They often believe they know more than the specialists who are involved in their treatment or care. This concept of terminal uniqueness is well known in the halls of Alcoholics Anonymous where most participants are often dual-diagnosed with more than one mental or emotional condition, including disordered personalities. They may not be understood by other people because the way they think is distorted and outside the norm.

Additionally, all of the people with these disorders display a diminished capacity for empathy while being manipulative and exploitive when trying to get what they want and need. If ever asked directly whether they operate in this manner, most would deny it. Some researchers still question whether the narcissist understands or even recognizes what he is doing and saying.

Personality disordered people hold others responsible for their life difficulties. They believe there is nothing wrong with them, and that is why they are also unable to recognize there is anything unacceptable about their behaviors. For many, it is possible that their way of operating in the world at large is truly all they know how to do and be. The common thread among these four disorders—antisocial, histrionic, borderline, and narcissistic—is that they all need a *narcissistic supply*. However, the methods they use to secure the attention, affections, and affirmation from others may vary, as you will see in the list below:

**Antisocial PD:** these individuals obtain their narcissistic supply from power, money, or anything else that gives them a sense of control over others. They often live on the edge, and the rush of this is their idea of fun—even if others are hurt in the process. They focus on getting negative attention, such as causing fear in others as a way of getting them to behave in ways they need, while gaining notoriety from their harmful behaviors.

**Histrionic PD:** flirtatious with expressions of a strong sexuality. They may feed on romantic and sexual encounters, flaunting the shape of their bodies through physical exercise and their focus on beauty. They can be quite seductive in their mannerisms in order to draw others toward them.

**Borderline PD:** these individuals suffer from extreme separation anxiety and are terribly frightened of abandonment. They form strong connections while engaging in sexual encounters as a means of not having to feel abandoned. They will allow themselves to be used and exploited in order to not be rejected and abandoned. We describe their thinking as very "black and white," a kind of all-or-nothing thinking.

## Treatment Expectations for Narcissistic Personality Disorder

Not unlike dealing with a drug addict or alcoholic who denies that his drinking or drug use is a problem for anyone but himself or the anorexic person who is wasting away before our eyes yet denies she has a problem, the person with NPD is in complete denial about the impact their abusive and demanding behaviors have on others.

However, Dr. Craig Malkin, key researcher in the field of narcissism research, gives us hope when he writes, "Yes, I do believe it's possible for people to change, even if they've been diagnosed with something as deeply entrenched and formidable as a personality disorder."[3]

Because narcissists use defenses such as ignoring, suppression, denial, projection, and disavowing their own vulnerability to avoid feeling exposed, change requires opening themselves to feel this same vulnerability that they have worked all their lives to keep at bay.

"It isn't that they can't change," Dr. Malkin says. "It's that it often threatens their sense of personhood to even try."[4]

The sad irony of the narcissistic condition is that, to protect themselves, narcissists inevitably invite the very rejection and abandonment they fear. The therapeutic work required for someone to gradually relinquish the defenses used to distance themselves from such intense pain is no small order. This is how the individual has survived over time. Even attempts at mildly altering their behavior is incredibly frightening because the emotional pain they have walled off is threatening to them. But the need to accept disowned parts of themselves is part of the healing process. Integrating these painful aspects of the self is paramount to a successful recovery. At that point, the individual no longer has a need for the compensatory behaviors.[5]

With these things in mind about the way a narcissist operates and what is required of him for healing, let's consider some previous examples. Think of Paul, who was only briefly mentioned earlier. He squandered his family fortune without the involvement of his wife, crashed the family business, and finally ended up homeless. When his wife divorced him, he went to his aging mother, asking to live in her guest house. While living there rent-free in exchange for getting his aging mother to appointments with her doctors, his selfish sense of entitlement caused him such dissatisfaction that he asked the family to pay for his gas mileage—even though the car he was using also belonged to his mother. He lost the love and affection of his entire extended family, including his wife and children.

Consider Dick, who lost the "love of his life" while settling for the love of money and the immature emotional support of a married adult child. His inability to be intimate with his adult wife of many years kept him at a distance for fear of being emotionally engulfed, just as his mother had done to him as a child and young teen. These examples give us a brief glimpse of the fear narcissists live with daily, resulting in their inability to participate fully in their own lives or to be present to the people closest to them.

Our greatest hope is that the natural consequences of the NPD's own behavior would create for them the need for intervention, whether personal or legal. However, this is rarely reported. Dr. Sheen Ambardar suggests considering the help of a professional interventionist, someone who is specifically trained to address the afflicted person regarding issues such as his not getting his needs met or not meeting his life goals.[6]

An interventionist can also help the family or spouse practice how to deal with the manipulative behaviors the narcissist uses to control people, such as twisting others' words to project blame for their own difficulties, interrupting, walking out, or reacting with rage when their own protective level of extreme sensitivity causes them to react with foul words, harsh criticisms, and threats to end the relationship by separation or divorce. These are examples of narcissistic injuries demonstrated by the narcissist when something threatens to expose him.

## Can Treatment Change the Narcissist?

The options identified here are recommended for individuals diagnosed with NPD. Most personality disordered people have additional co-existing disorders, so a combination of psychother-apy and medication is routinely found to be most beneficial. The syndromes most frequently found to accompany NPD include substance/alcohol dependency, anxiety, depression, ADHD, impulsivity disorder, bipolar disorder, and eating disorders. It is not uncommon to find that people with NPD may also demonstrate characteristics of the other three personality disorders in Cluster B: histrionic, borderline, and antisocial.[7]

Eating disorders in their various forms also include a form of narcissistic behavior. Says one treatment center director, "Narcissism is a form of pathological functioning that drives the individual to be obsessed with their own importance, beauty, status or body image combined with insensitivity or compassion for others. People with disordered patterns of eating are equally pathologically absorbed with their own body image, diets, exer-cise habits, to the exclusion of most everything and everyone in their lives." Some research has identified that the characteristics of bulimics match up closely with NPDs.[8, 9]

One study determined that narcissists have two types of internal voices. One voice is the self-aggrandizing and self-soothing voice of the anti-self; the second voice is paradoxical, representing the self with low self-esteem, and a self-hating, self-demeaning inner voice. This description is characteristic of the eating disordered individual, especially the anorexic who perceives a compliment like, "You look really good," as a critical remark that may set off a cascade of narcis-sistic injury, which then triggers a desperate attempt to regain control by restricting food intake. They might respond with a condescend-ing remark to restore their depleted self-esteem.[10]

If others could only understand that narcissistic inflation really reflects the extent to which an individual fears feeling small and insufficient, then we all might better appreciate the plight of the narcissist. The pathogenesis of pathological personality characteristics is about how individuals have survived their own pain.[11]

We may see variable levels of intensity in the individual's personality style, but as previously mentioned, narcissism is an enduring character style. With enough insight, motivation, and self-awareness, it may be possible for the narcissist, through psychotherapy, to make some adjustments. However, it rarely resolves the problem long-term. Typically, their behaviors re-emerge later. This is important when considering the distinctions between narcissism and bipolar disorder. Narcissism is an enduring disorder of the personality and does not abate and return from time to time.[12] Bipolar disorder can be managed with stress reduction techniques, psychotherapy, and medication management. Bipolar individuals can experience periods of significant remission.

Larry, one of my narcissistic clients, describes himself as a high-powered sales executive with a glowing background of huge sales success with a major international manufacturing firm. When I asked him to clarify what might be going on that would precipitate a call for counseling, he said, "Oh, I went to see my doctor for a tune-up, and he thought it might be good to see a counselor, so he sent me to you." When Larry first arrived at my office, he was dressed sharply in business casual dress, had a big friendly smile on his face, and took a seat as near to me as he could get. And that's a bit surprising for a first-time visit.

As we began to talk, Larry was filled with information about his handsome family (all successful college graduates), his perfect marriage of thirty years, and descriptions of his many great friends. Yet none of what he shared described his reason for coming. With no indication of anything but good news, he then said he'd been bedridden for the past three weeks with severe depression and debilitating anxiety that threatened to keep him housebound.

"Has anything recently changed in your life?" I asked. At my question, his whole demeanor changed into a mixture of anger, rage, and talk of retaliation. Yet his words didn't match the few tears he fought to hold back.

"I got fired from my job! It's not fair. My sales numbers have been astronomical," he said in a loud voice, leaning toward me as if to guarantee I would be intimidated enough to automatically agree with him. "I've led a team of top sales execs over the past five years, and now they do this to me! I'm planning to sue them for age discrimination, and I know I can win this one. I always win!"

Our time was now up, and we hadn't even gotten to how I could help him. I invited him to reschedule to try to address the depression and anxiety with some skill-building strategies that might help with both. Although he returned several weeks later, his focus was clearly not on gaining skills. Larry only wanted to focus on the team of experts he'd assembled to fight his case. When I asked if he'd returned to see his doctor, he claimed he was too busy with the attorneys working on his case. It seemed he could only pay lip service to the fact that "he was in control of this thing now and didn't believe counseling could be of help to him."

Sadly, Larry's haughty, intimidating manner, along with a demonstrated belief system that was inflexible, helped define a few of the important characteristics that make it difficult to maintain a close relationship with a narcissist. They rarely seek counseling unless the accompanying symptoms can be addressed quickly. Sadly, Larry didn't want to explore any of the real reasons he might have been let go. He never returned to my office again.

His fear of feeling vulnerable—especially considering he chose to assume the company made their decision based on his advancing age—made it seem obvious that he was unable to accept that fact of life. Despite the company's need to update systems to meet the times, Larry could only blame the firm for something he truly feared within himself; he was no longer needed in his work, and his children were now married and had left home. What might have been viewed as a natural life transition was devastating for Larry. Instead, he experienced his job loss as having the rug pulled out from under him.

Narcissists are often lonely, have superficial relationships, possess an extreme fear of failure, and may suffer with significant anxiety, just as Larry did. Only when their relationships or employment have been significantly impacted might they consider some form of treatment. NPDs on the extreme end of the continuum are often poor candidates for therapeutic change.

However, those who display annoying, hurtful, or damaging traits in their interpersonal relationships may find their way into treatment because a spouse has threatened to leave them.

Another important example of narcissistic thinking and actions was revealed as Hal and Linda came to their initial intake session. Hal called ahead, lamenting about all the ways Linda wasn't "into" their marriage anymore. When they arrived for the appointment, Hal pulled out his list of all Linda's failings as a wife. He clearly believed she was the cause of all their marital difficulties. Hal believed himself to be a serious Christian, having previously pastored a small country church.

But now he heralded his own efforts to "take care of his family," despite having not worked outside the home for the previous eight years. Linda worked a fifty-hour week at her job, carried the family health plan, paid down the mortgage, and helped two daughters attend college. Hal left his last job in a huff because he believed the work was beneath his skill set. He was clearly not being appreciated by his family or superiors for all he could bring to the table. He decided on his own to be the house husband, choosing to stay home with their teenage daughters, who, according to him, needed supervision.

Linda sat almost speechless as she listened to Hal talk about her failings. Even though she had kept the family afloat all these years, Hal gave her no credit for her contributions to their marriage. Hal quickly decided they could only afford for one of them to come for treatment, and since Linda was the one to blame and needed the most help, she should stay in counseling. The therapist quickly recognized the opportunity to strongly encourage Linda's return.

Within a few visits, Linda openly described Hal's controlling behaviors, attempts to isolate her, gaslighting behaviors to make her believe she was crazy, and examples of emotional violence and verbal abuse. Hal routinely talked with his daughters about their mother's failings as a wife, including details about the couple's lack of sexual intimacy, which Hal openly conveyed to his young daughters as something that all wives owe their husbands. Hal, a type of spiritual narcissist, was often found using scriptural passages to support his own distorted beliefs, which he utilized as a means of controlling his wife and daughters. As a result, both daughters aligned with their dad for a time to avoid his painful rejection, which he threatened regularly in his spiritual lectures.

Linda made several attempts to separate from Hal, searching for some measure of emotional safety. Each time, he would pull her back in with lies and manipulative promises. If she didn't comply, he threatened that she risked permanently losing her children. Linda was sure she was losing her mind.

In the end, Hal's wife moved out and filed for divorce. His eldest daughter was so distraught about his actions toward her and her mother that she moved away from the family. With all of these consequences, he was still unable to take responsibility for any part of the tearing apart of his family. He eventually turned to his younger, newly married daughter to maintain some level of narcissistic supply. As a result, she was forced by a manipulating father to abandon her relationship with her older sibling as well as her mother in order to not be abandoned by her own father.

You can see through these many examples that the choice for change on the part of the narcissist is very difficult and challenging. It defies the very way he has learned to live his life—even if it means he risks the complete loss of anything and anyone who might hold meaning and have affection, compassion, and empathy for him as a person.

## Treatment Goals for the NPD Person

Hold on here while not yet giving up all hope. Depending upon where the disorder falls on the diagnostic continuum, it is possible the narcissist in your life may find his way into some form of treatment, even if under duress. Should a family opt for an intervention to address even a co-occurring disorder like alcohol abuse, severe depression, or anger management, it is possible for some change to occur, if only in the narcissist's mind, to secure more of what may be important to him. Consider the following as some of the primary treatment goals:

1. Learn to become more empathic to the rights, feelings, needs, and emotions of others. The NPD person does not and cannot self-reflect without help because that risks a level of vulnerability that he has worked to avoid at all costs.

2. Help the NPD recognize and understand how their negative patterns of thinking and behavior are distorted and result in the consequences they experience, such as employment, relationships, marriages, and children.

3. Identify how these distortions prevent them from getting what they want most in life, while sometimes even creating what they're trying to avoid.

4. Aid them in understanding that others are separate people with rights, needs, and desires of their own. Others also have feelings they need and want to express. It does not mean the

narcissist directly caused these. He may need to
learn to tolerate hearing them.

5. Teach boundary-setting skills to address many
of the destructive, manipulative behaviors and
maneuvers they use to control others.[13]

## Suggested Treatment Interventions for NPD

Should a narcissist find himself in a position to consider some
form of treatment, there are many options available. Whatever
interventions are considered, it might be important to hear that
approaching a narcissist in psychotherapy is a complex endeavor.
A large range of variables exists that makes the process different
for everyone. Talk therapy, called psychotherapy, is the most useful treatment. The goals of treatment are to help NPDs learn to
relate to others better so their relationships are more intimate,
enjoyable, and rewarding. Helping individuals understand where
their emotions come from while helping them understand their
problems are internal and not necessarily caused by other people
or situations is an invaluable goal of treatment. Educating them
about their own drives to compete, their inherent lack of trust and
the problems that arise out of this, and how much they despise
themselves can all be beneficial goals of therapy.[14]

Psychiatry professionals have seen that some NPD clients
enter therapy to have their narcissistic wounds soothed rather than
to actually seek change in their lives and relationships. Therapists
working with NPDs need to determine early in the treatment
process whether the person really wants to get better or whether
the narcissist is seeking a new way to feed his narcissistic supply.[15]

The following includes a brief overview of the specialized forms of treatment that can be explored as part of any treatment plan.

**Dialectical Behavioral Therapy (DBT)**—a method used for treating people involved in intensely destructive behaviors, has been found effective for some personality disorders, eating disorders, and substance-use disorders. A three-step process walks clients through ways to re-frame their negative self-talk into more life-enhancing directives. Thinking positively results in changed feelings, leading them toward greater flexibility of choices for action.[16]

**Cognitive Behavioral Therapy (CBT)**—Because the person with NPD rarely sees that there is anything wrong with the way they think, act, and behave toward others, CBT may help them understand how what they think determines how they feel and how their feelings drive their actions. One of the goals of CBT would be to help the narcissist see how their lack of empathy and inflated self-centeredness could be problematic. Although they may not care how their actions affect those around them, helping them discover ways their actions prevent them from gaining what they want might open the door to some trust building.

When narcissists are facing a life crisis like divorce, loss of job, loss of career position, or some failure resulting in financial loss, an important question to ask the NPD person is whether they really want any help. No one else can decide for another individual whether their choices are based upon unwillingness or inability. How the NPD individual answers this question will determine how others respond to him. Consider the example of the couple that follows.[17]

John and Sally married after a lifetime of friendship. Remarried for nine years now, John appeared more staunchly self-focused and self-serving than Sally had ever experienced him to be. As a last resort before filing for divorce and purchasing a condo on her own, she asked John directly whether he was willing to make any adjustments she had requested to improve their marriage. John sat silently without any expression and stated, "I really don't see what's so bad in our marriage that you need to leave, but if that's what you want, I won't stop you." Sally's heart was broken when she realized she meant so little to him after so many years. And in John's defense, he truly could not comprehend his wife's actions.

John's identification in his statement "I really don't see what's so bad in our marriage that you need to leave" was revealing John's distorted thinking. He was unable to get out of his own thinking long enough to see his wife's position. He couldn't relinquish his own focus on himself long enough to see or hear her pain. Because he took no responsibility to make any adjustment toward preventing the decision Sally was making, he felt little if any emotion about her leaving—believing her choice to be completely hers and hers alone. CBT would have helped John see that his distorted thinking set him up to maintain a level of emotional distance that destroyed his marriage. At that point, being right was more important to him than saving his marriage.

**Group Therapy**—Group therapy requires individuals to learn patience, to understand and demonstrate empathy and compassion for others, and to be present to listen to others while becoming less self-focused. Studies have identified the long-term group process can benefit NPD persons by providing them with a safe-haven experience in which they can explore boundaries with help, receive and offer appropriate feedback to others, and develop trusting relationships over time, all while increasing their own self-awareness and self-esteem. This same process has helped both addicts and alcoholics who often have narcissistic tendencies.[18]

**Medication Assessment and Intervention**—There are no specific medications used to treat NPD. Because it is a personality disorder, there is no definitive biochemical basis for its development. The symptoms of co-occurring disorders may be identified and treated with drug therapy to help reduce or alleviate some of the most common conditions such as depression, anxiety, ADHD or ADD, and other mood disorders like bipolar, emotional stress, and sleeplessness.

Various categories of drug therapy may be utilized that can help produce a calming effect, improve impulse control, reduce symptoms of anger and rage, and lessen sensitivity to hostility and rejection. These medications should be used in conjunction with psychotherapy.

For some people, the therapies we have addressed may be inadequate or even inappropriate. For others, these options may only be the starting point in their treatment plan.

## Alternative Therapies to Consider

### Eye-Movement Desensitization and Reprocessing—(EMDR).

EMDR has been particularly useful for people who have experienced trauma in their past. It requires no talk therapy or medication. Because early life trauma is believed to be a factor in the development of NPD, this method helps the individual put the trauma of the past behind them. Unlike more conventional therapies, the process uses a person's rhythmic eye movements while being guided by the therapist performing the treatment. The side-to-side rhythmic scanning seems to erase traumatic memories from the brain in a fashion that allows the individual to move beyond these emotionally charged memories. Some success has been reported with the technique.[19]

**Rapid Resolution Therapy—(RRT).** RRT is another brain-based approach for the treatment of stored trauma imprints in the limbic system or emotional brain. These brain-based methods help identify the root of the emotional conflict in the hope of inducing change. The emotional brain stores the early fight-flight-freeze trauma reactions and returns to these, like open computer programs operating without our awareness, when we are triggered by similar events or situations. The reactions are typical of what we identify as Post-Traumatic Stress Disorder. NPD people are exquisitely sensitive to external sources that could reactivate original trauma. Although there is nothing required of the individual in the moment, the brain continues to churn out old traumatic thoughts, sensations, and feelings that are no longer useful but seem to demand the individual take some specific action, even when there is no current action to be taken.

Although the methods used are quite unique, they seem to help free the energy used by the brain by creating new pathways, which help to eliminate destructive reactions previously generated by the brain. Whether the NPD person is aware of their own early trauma, or even if what they did experience didn't seem traumatic at the time, this method may offer great potential for change since it does not require in-depth talk therapy.[20]

**Twelve-Step Programs**—"Came to believe that a power greater than ourselves could restore us to sanity."

Twelve-Step Programs were created to help those suffering with addictive patterns of living. The steps of the program and attendance at group meetings help individuals identify how their lives may be out of control and unmanageable because many of the behaviors they use are damaging both to themselves and to others. An important concept for the NPD individual to grasp is that his words and actions can truly harm other people.

Grasping the spiritual concept of letting go of control by turning the outcome over to a greater power rather than over to another person might be a gentler way of introducing this difficult concept, which the narcissist may have trouble understanding. Taking a fearless and searching moral inventory, another step in the program, might encourage the NPD person to recognize ways his attitudes and behaviors do not work to get his needs met. Feeling a real sense of comfort and connection helps him begin to feel a sense of personal worth and value as others affirm them for coming back.[21]

Celebrate Recovery is a Christian-based Twelve-Step Program usually found in larger churches. Much like Alcoholics Anonymous and Al-Anon, everyone can find a place in this program that offers scriptural support for change with God at the helm rather than the concept of a Higher Power.

## Spiritual Renewal

Although some would consider spiritual renewal an alternative treatment, I believe it would be a necessary adjunctive therapy since the basic foundational roots of this disorder may have had their earliest beginnings at the Fall of Mankind. Since it is generally thought that the Twelve Step Process used for healing addicts, alcoholics, and other addictive and compulsive behaviors is a God-inspired program for healing, it seems important to consider other Christian-based programs focused on healing human brokenness.

In this regard, New Life Ministry is a national Christian ministry that offers three-day retreat weekends in multiple major U.S. cities throughout the year. The programs are a combination of Bible-based talks on specific topics related to many of the life issues that couples encounter. *Every Man's Battle* is offered for men who struggle with infidelity issues in their marriages and relationships. *Restored* is a program designed specifically for women who have experienced infidelity in their marriages. *Ultimate Intimacy* is a couple's program designed for couples who are struggling with multiple marital concerns. An additional healing weekend is based upon author Steve Arterburn's newest book: *Take Your Life Back.* Whether attended jointly or individually, these weekends are created to engender hope, healing, and freedom through the healing power of Jesus Christ in our lives.

If a narcissist finds himself at a point in time in which he risks losing everything meaningful to him, it is possible he might be open to the idea that he could consider letting go of his need to control people, places, things, and substances in his life. If attendance would even open the door to this very concept, it might be worth considering attendance as an option as part of the narcissist's treatment plan.

## Stress Reduction Techniques

Practices such as yoga, tai chi, and prayer may help increase self-awareness and slow one's pace, focusing on the body and breathing. This can help change both thinking and perceiving. Mindfulness training practices that include stress reduction techniques may also be useful. Stress reduction involves helping the client identify what seems to be causing him stress.

If depression and/or anxiety are present, it is wise to treat these with small doses of targeted medications at first while psychotherapy is ongoing. If the client is unable to see the destructive results of his behavior, the focus on reducing the stress that builds inside him, resulting in socially unacceptable behaviors, can be explored.

Because NPD is not a biologically determined disorder, research is limited regarding how healthy eating and regular exercise benefit the disorder. However, knowing that multiple other co-occurring disorders accompany NPD, eating right, getting plenty of rest, and recreation do a body good.

## Long-Term Outpatient Treatment

Long-term outpatient care is recommended if a therapeutic relationship can be established. Overall, this approach involves a combination of therapies to address co-existing disorders like anxiety, depression, ADHD, impulsivity, mood disorders, and disordered eating practices. Medications may be used for co-occurring disorders, though no medications are available to treat NPD. If an NPD patient becomes a threat to himself or others, shorter hospital stays are useful for stabilization of environmental stressors, adjustment, and monitoring of medications.[22] Directly confronting damaging behaviors by identifying and naming them can provide soothing relief after they are exposed. Reality therapy is a type of therapy used only in an inpatient setting.[23]

It is vitally important to address several significant facts about the NPD person in your life. Their addictive use of a long list of behaviors and substances is utilized to numb or mask and maintain denial of their intense internal level of emotional pain and their destructive thought loops. Those NPDs on the extreme end of the continuum are so entirely self-focused that it is nearly impossible to achieve and maintain any level of true intimacy in a relationship.

And finally, it is difficult to know for certain whether increased stress has any affect upon their behavior and thinking. It would seem reasonable to consider that anything that changes their schedule, routine, or plans would likely increase the possibility for a narcissistic injury followed by intense words and behavior. However, psychotherapy for NPDs requires a therapist who emphasizes empathy and does not confront people who demonstrate extreme entitlement or an exaggerated sense of self-worth and self-importance.

# CHAPTER 5

# Boundary Setting Skills with the Narcissist

Boundaries describe the ways we bring things into our lives and how we keep other things out, especially in our relationships. Boundaries are necessary for identifying personal space, ideas, thoughts, desires, bodies, etc., yet not everyone recognizes them or understands the need for them. When dealing with NPDs across the spectrum of severity, personal boundaries often don't exist. That's why you need to learn how to define, express, and establish them for yourself. The narcissist's distorted perceptions cause him to see others as extensions of himself. He believes others exist to help him get his personal needs and desires met to the exclusion of even thinking that you or anyone else around him might have their own goals and agenda.

I would imagine that if you've been involved with a narcissist for very long, you might have been told that your ideas aren't worth much or to keep them to yourself. But most of all, the NPD often manages the lives of those around him by controlling with fear. When you're afraid, it's difficult to try anything new, reach out to others, ask for help outside your circumstances, or risk being vulnerable yourself, fearing you won't be believed or taken seriously.

Hear me say right now you must "step out of the boat." Jesus didn't call Peter to step out of the boat and walk on water because He wanted him to be afraid and sink. Jesus called him and told Peter to keep his eyes on the Lord. The same is true here. You need to take actions that the narcissist in your life will not like, accept, or even support. He might rail against you to stop. Had Peter never risked taking that first step of faith, he might never have fulfilled God's purpose for his life. Imagining Peter's attempt to walk on water reminds us that we are not in total control of our lives no matter what our circumstances are. Yet if we keep our focus on Jesus, even when we feel like we're going under, He promises to never leave us or forsake us. What a comfort to our souls!

For this reason, it is imperative for you to develop your own voice, and you also need to ask yourself some important questions. What do you want your life as an individual to look like? You will no doubt begin to realize there are differences between you and the narcissist in your life. However, until you discover your own interests, talents, and gifts, you'll never know what's possible.

Christ commands us to love all people—even those who are our enemies. We all fall short of the mark set out for us, so who among us can boast? Think of the wounds Christ bore for all of us when He went to the cross. Your journey toward freedom will be a difficult journey but not an impossible one. But Jesus is asking you to step out of the boat. If you continue to live your life around the NPD person, doing what you have been doing, I promise you will suffer more of the same pain, disappointment, shame, guilt, loneliness, invisibility, and insignificance. Instead, I encourage you to consider changing your actions and reactions.

We all know this is certainly not an easy thing to do. When you have been lied to, experienced broken promises, and been discounted, ignored, and betrayed in multiple ways, Scripture tells us to turn the other cheek, pay back more than was taken, go the extra mile, make amends first, and more. That's easy to say—but hard to do! And it cannot be done alone. Remember, what will be suggested for you to do is not for the other person's benefit. It's for your benefit. If the narcissist in your life benefits, that's a win-win situation. However, do not expect him to change just because you change. Ultimately, you will be asked to forgive the narcissist's actions and behaviors toward you, but in the meantime, you have your own work to do.

## Rules of Engagement with NPD People

Having a guide to help you track where you're going is important. So, let's take a quick look at what emotional health looks like:

- Being able to move beyond our past with a solid sense of who we are in the world.
- Experiencing a level of emotional stability that allows us to be able to meet daily challenges and grow through them.
- We're secure in knowing that relationships are not only important, they are also necessary for our ongoing sense of connection and belonging in the world.

- Our reality is relatively free from distortions, and we feel free to share this reality with others without shame, guilt, criticism, or judgment.
- We're able to focus on more positives, and while we search for the best, we do not reach for perfection as our top priority.
- Our strong faith has helped us understand the meaning of what it is to become whole, with a life filled with purpose, meaning, and hope. We know that in a personal relationship with God, through his Son Jesus Christ, we can feel good about who we are and whose we are. In that place, we feel most alive and fulfilled.

Clearly, this may sound like utopia to you right now. However, this is simply a description of the direction you are headed in this healing process. It's important to hear at the outset that if you, your child, or someone you love is experiencing some form of abuse, neglect, or being used by the narcissist to fulfill his own needs, it is vital that you take the necessary action steps to stop this damaging behavior as soon as possible. It might be important to be reminded here that narcissism seems to run in families. If you are responsible for the care of children or you happened to be a child of a narcissistic parent, you know only too well how imperative it is that you seek help for yourself and your children. Remember that you may be called to advocate on someone else's behalf. If so, you will clearly need a whole community of supporters to accomplish this.

In their award-winning book *Boundaries*, Henry Cloud and John Townsend define boundaries as "where you begin and end" and the same for the other.[1] We often assume that if we're in a relationship, we have the same feelings, attitudes, behaviors, choices, and values. No so! Our relationships in Christ are based upon having the *freedom* to be the person Christ created us to become. And in relationship with a narcissist, that may look and feel very different.

If we come from family systems in which our boundaries were constantly being violated—such as being told what we liked or didn't like, being told how to think and feel about specific things, and having attitudes and ways of treating others modeled for us that we knew were not right—boundary violations occurred. These kinds of personal violations are some of the most important issues that cause distress and disharmony in relationships and in marriages.

I often tell clients that when the person you are dealing with has little knowledge of boundaries, you will feel as though you are stretching yourself so far out on a limb trying to establish boundaries that you may feel guilty at first for even attempting to make the change. What you're doing requires risk. It's risky to speak clearly and firmly to someone you fear might reject you, withdraw from your relationship, or even retaliate. Establishing boundaries is never easy, whether with family, friends, spouses, or children.[2]

## Gentle Confrontation—Basic Ways to Begin

A basic confrontation formula sounds a little like the example that follows. What's important to consider is this: just because you express yourself calmly and firmly doesn't mean that the other person will agree, like what you're offering, or even understand the purpose of what you're doing. This formula is for you to express yourself and find your own voice. It is possible that any form of confrontation with a person who is narcissistic may not be a wise choice. Be certain to address this with a supporter and/or have someone with you when you attempt this process:

When you_____ (tell me this, do this, say that I _____, etc.) I feel_____ (sad, angry, hurt, discounted, diminished, unimportant, insignificant).

When I feel this way (sad, ashamed, hurt, belittled, etc.), I do this_____ (leave, withdraw, run away, emotionally shut down, fight back). Because this doesn't help our connection at all, what I'd like to ask of you is this_____ (would you be willing to stop, change, alter, tell me, consider)?

Wait for a response from the other person as a form of commitment to the process. If you need to repeat the request, do it one more time.

We need our feelings to help us identify when something needs to change. If you are angry, hurt, or feel negative and ashamed because someone has behaved in a certain way toward you, it is your responsibility to do something about it. Here's an example of what I'm talking about:

When Cindy planned a great dinner for herself and her husband, Ryan, even making plans for the children to stay overnight at Grandma's, and Ryan showed up two hours late without a call, Cindy was not only worried, she was now seething with anger since this wasn't the first time he had done this. She was angry that her husband's thoughtlessness could raise such ire in her, but she realized she had to be responsible to address her feelings about it with Ryan.

What healthy boundary setting says is that we all have disappointments over our unfulfilled desires. Other people cannot make us feel a certain way. This is difficult to swallow! In fact, many of us literally choke on this one! And we can't punish others for not getting what we want, especially if we haven't identified for the other person in advance what we are hoping for. Conflict arises because we each want different things for ourselves. Problems arise when we fail to initially establish limits, as well as when we fail to clarify our personal needs and wants.

Since this had previously happened to our couple, Cindy needed to ask Ryan to commit to being home within a time range. If he believed he couldn't or didn't want to do this because he preferred to go out with his buddies after work, he needed to tell Cindy in advance. It didn't mean he didn't want to spend time with her. Instead, it meant he wanted to make his own plans, but he hadn't shared this with Cindy. Blaming him only caused distance between them.

Consequences demonstrate the law of reaping and sowing. Whatever we focus on, we'll get more of. If I worry and fret, over time, I will surely worry and fret more. If I worry about something someone said about me or about what will happen because I did or said something, my worry and anxiety will do nothing to change the situation. It will only consume more of my time, energy, and attention. Nothing will change.

Remember that consequences are not punishments. It is important not to identify consequences after a boundary has been violated. Do not argue about the boundary you set. Narcissists feed off your angry energy, so when they upset you enough that you act out, they'll come in with the left hook and tell you "You're crazy." Or they'll blame you for the outcome. Remember, be clear and concise about what you are asking for.

Now consider this example of the need for boundary setting. Imagine that Sharon is constantly critical of everything she asks Rick to do for her. Eventually, Rick will feel there's nothing he can do or say that will make Sharon happy. Rick loves his wife, but he doesn't love her nagging dissatisfaction. Instead, he feels like a "puppet on a string," needing to jump every time Sharon speaks.

Sharon and Rick need to set boundaries to improve their marital communication. Sharon needs to realize that Rick is not obligated to accept her criticism and demeaning remarks. With help from a trained therapist, Rick came to understand that until he takes the lead and tells Sharon how demeaned and disrespected he feels when she tries to control him, he is responsible for "reaping what he sows." By allowing Sharon to continue to be critical, judgmental, and ungrateful, little will change.

Instead, sharing his feelings with Sharon and asking for her to stop giving him negative feedback after everything he does for her would help improve communication significantly. If she has questions or concerns, she is free to voice those ahead of time. Rick needs to communicate to Sharon that he would like her to support his good-hearted willingness to save them money by allowing him to do the things around the house he can do without being judged or criticized.

It is vital in close relationships that people share some basic thoughts and feelings about important areas of life where boundary violations are most likely to occur. Authors Cloud and Townsend refer to this as "the law of exposure."[3] Passive boundaries can be extremely damaging to the relationship when they are not clearly identified. They can lead to withdrawal, triangulation, pouting, affairs, and other passive-aggressive behaviors.

Some of the key areas in a relationship where clear, concise communication must be established early are skin and bodies, words, physical space, time, emotional distance, other relationships, and consequences. When we speak of the marital relationship, we refer to Christ's admonition to the church regarding how to behave with one another.

But Ephesians 5:28–29 is often taken out of context and misinterpreted.[4] Wives are not to be submissive slaves to husbands, operating under their control and domination. Husbands are instructed to love their wives as Christ loves the church and to sacrifice for them in the same way. Wives should treat their husbands with the same love, honor, and respect given to them. Marriage is a partnership.

## The Process of Establishing Boundaries with the Narcissist

We've been talking about the difficulty most people have in establishing boundaries in relationships, even when narcissism isn't present. When narcissism is a part of the relationship dynamic, it's even more difficult to set boundaries—yet even more important to try and to take the risk! If you are in relationship with a personality disordered individual, it is imperative to take back your life by seeking help and direction. A Christian therapist can show you how to take charge of your own thoughts, actions, and behaviors to become a new creation in Christ. As we've previously identified, narcissists have few if any boundaries for themselves and resist others setting them. With that in mind, it is important to proceed on your own behalf with the helpful support of others you can trust. Some helpful suggestions follow:[5]

> 1. If you're feeling bad about who you are or about the kind of life you're living with the NPD person, plan to put some space between the two of you.
>
> 2. Listen to your body and become more skilled at identifying your own feelings, thoughts, and needs. This requires practice and patience.
>
> 3. Gain clarity about what part of the problems really are about you, and what part belongs to the narcissist. Begin to see yourself as a separate person who is equally capable of behaving in ways that can harm others.
>
> 4. Clearly identify and express in simple words those acts you will no longer allow to be directed toward you, while sharing the consequences you will impose when you feel violated. It might be important to remember that the narcissist has his own agenda, which rarely changes regardless of how kind, compassionate, helpful, or loving you are. Your focus needs not to be on how to change him. It is about taking your life back!
>
> 5. Focus on safety first—for you and any minor children. Accept the possibility that you may need

to remove yourself and your children from this relationship to guard your emotional, physical, sexual, and spiritual safety.

6. Learn about the psychological strategies of emotional detachment, while educating yourself about enmeshment, especially if you are sharing the same environment. Finding yourself trying to figure out what the narcissist is thinking or planning is mentally and emotionally exhausting. Conserve this energy to focus on what you want and need.

7. Accept that defeat is possible, although the process is not about winning. You cannot help or fix anyone who does not want help. Grieve the loss of what you hoped your life would be like.

8. Learn to manage your own feelings of vulnerability by securing outside help from a counselor, pastor, trusted friend, or spiritual mentor. Narcissists are easily triggered by your expressed vulnerability, while projecting onto you what they are most fearful of for themselves.

9. Less is more. Stop discussing your personal issues with the narcissist. Identify trustworthy outside support.

10. When things are calm and there's no current drama, it might be important to take time for yourself. Find your own space for a time. Narcissists are known for creating conflict when

they become bored. Remember, they live on adrenaline, so it is difficult for them to relax.

11. Establish clear physical, emotional, mental, or spiritual boundaries for yourself. Remove yourself from a situation before you feel pushed to your limit.[6]

12. "Guard your heart with all diligence, for out of it is the wellspring of life."[7] Recognize that family, friends, children, and spouses in their disordered state are willing to hurt you if they feel the need to protect themselves from exposure.

13. Learn to identify and recognize the tricks, games, and tactics that narcissists use to control others. Once you understand what these are, you can stand firmly against them. "A malicious man disguises himself with his lips, but in his heart he harbors deceit."[8]

14. Seriously consider the "no contact" rule when there are no minor children involved. This means no texting, emails, calls, letters, in-person meetings (publicly or privately), and no yelling. This strategy is useful when activity in the relationship has become toxic and your safety is at risk. I would suggest legal consultation to be assured you are within your legal rights to do this.

15. When minor children are involved, special email accounts can be established with walls of protection built in. It is a way of limiting all but

essential or emergency contacts. It allows you to document rude, indecent, threatening, and demeaning remarks directed toward you without your needing to respond immediately or with emotion.

16. Learn to communicate in a brief, concise format, being careful to monitor your voice, tone, and attitude. Responding in a benign fashion without emotion is best.

17. Should communication escalate and you feel unsafe or overwhelmed, leave the room. However, always be aware of the location of your car keys in the event you need to leave altogether. Have a bag packed and a place to go for safety at any time of day or night. Do not be afraid to call 911 for additional help.

18. Remember that the rules of engagement with a narcissist include being firm and sticking to what you say. Practice communicating clearly and directly. If you become emotional or make a mistake, step aside, regroup with help, and then move forward with both support and prayer and greater resolve to not be demeaning in your words with the narcissist.

19. Be truthful and accountable for any part of your interaction that you can identify and own. It is very difficult to stand firm in the face of a perceived threat or repetitive attempt at

manipulation. Each time you stand firm, you have moved a giant step forward toward gaining your emotional freedom.

I hope this list has instilled hope in you, the kind of hope that no matter how the narcissistic individual approaches you, you now understand that you are not the problem! The NPD person has a serious disorder that he may not be able to recognize. The truth is that the behaviors and tactics he uses to get others to do what he wants are destructive, damaging, and may be representative of how he feels and thinks of himself. With this in mind, retaliation in any form will serve only to cause greater separation in the relationship. Using a few of the examples below may benefit both you and the narcissist.

## Speaking Truth in Love

One of the most important boundary-setting skills you will be learning to use is your voice.

The narcissists in our lives often control with fear, causing us to do one of two things: either retreat in fear and shut down emotionally while keeping thoughts and feelings to ourselves or vent openly in an effort to defend ourselves. Either way generally does not bring about a favorable outcome, so speaking the truth in love is a method to help you say what needs to be said without injuring the other person. Remember that you can only express yourself with the best possible motives—you cannot control the response of the other person.

1. Use "I" words as often as possible to defuse defensiveness, aggressiveness, and rage. For example:

"I find your comments hurtful" rather than "You are insensitive and rude to say that."[9]

2. Compliment the narcissist as you set boundaries. When narcissists are pleased with themselves, they may be enjoyable to be around. If you can offer a well-timed compliment, it may help bolster a sagging ego enough for them to see the benefit in the boundary you're trying to set. Instead of saying, "I told you to stop calling me so much. It interrupts my day!" a gentler, kinder response might be, "When you call me occasionally, it brightens my day."[10] By now I hope you know that you are not the cause of all his problems. Working toward this detached stance can be very beneficial.[11]

3. Affirm and recognize the narcissist's concerns and expectations. You might even briefly repeat them back to him to show that you are listening. Validating another's experience reduces the possibility for defensive or adversarial reactions. You do not need to agree or endorse what he's telling you. But acknowledging his demands in a respectful way will more likely be received positively than saying something with both attitude and tone, i.e., "You've got to be kidding me!" or "You expect me to own that?" Consider a more reflective response like "So I hear you saying that you think I'm the one who dropped

the ball. My perspective is quite different, so I'm not comfortable taking full responsibility for this situation." Or you might respond with, "I hear what you're saying; however, my view of the situation is different."[12]

4. Create a "win-win" situation when dealing with a boss or authority figure. Consider an option like this: "I understand that you need this job completed today. However, my schedule is already so full, I don't know how I can possibly get to it that quickly. I trust that you can see the dilemma this presents. I believe I can have it ready by—" (give a specific time and ask whether that might work).[13]

There are many and various ways of establishing boundaries, although communicating with a narcissistic individual presents challenges. They generally are not interested in what you say or think. If you can remember that their agenda is what they are focused on, challenging them in any way is rarely a good choice. Questioning them regarding how they came up with a thought, idea, or opinion is likely to cause the NPD to feel attacked—a word they often use when being questioned by others. As we move forward, let's take a closer look at how a few scenarios play out using these guidelines.

# CHAPTER 6

# Practical Helps That Can't Hurt

Forgive yourself for the blindness that put you in the path of those who betrayed you. Sometimes a good heart doesn't see the bad.[1]

Let's revisit the story of one of the clients I introduced you to earlier in this reading. We talked briefly about Janet's description of her own emotionally dependent behavior pattern that kept her in an intensely abusive lifetime relationship with a mother who had multiple co-occurring disorders in addition to being narcissistic.

Janet's mother was an alcoholic, narcissistic woman who developed bipolar disorder later in her life. Originally adopted into a family that took great care of her mother, Janet's mother never seemed satisfied. Always searching for more, she married quite young to leave her adoptive family. Her daughter Janet reported to me, "Clearly, my mother wasn't interested in having children. She never took care of us." In fact, she often left Janet and her twin sister, Janie, alone at the age of eight. Two years later, the girls were responsible for a two-year-old baby brother at night when their mother would frequent the bars while her father was working.

Janet remembers huddling together in one bed on cold nights, while having to hear their mother in her bedroom with men they never saw before. Mother's denial kept her separated from the aching hearts of her children who were desperate for her love. When any crisis occurred, their mother checked herself into the local mental hospital, where she would stay for a few days of rest. The girls raised themselves and their brother.

Janet came to see me after eighteen years of taking care of her now eighty-four-year-old mother. Her mother had also been diagnosed with bipolar disorder, but she refused to take her medication regularly and seemed incapable of making choices for her own self-care.

It was time for Janet to secure guardianship over her mother since the neighbors regularly called the police to stop the woman's disturbing behaviors like running through local lawns in her underwear. By this time, Janet's strong Christian faith raised such conflict within her that she needed help. Janet's own health had been seriously impacted by the chronic "walking on eggshells" characteristic of the trauma response of PTSD. She had gained weight, had high blood pressure, and was borderline diabetic.

"What do I do?" she cried tearfully. "She did nothing for us as little girls, and now I've been charged with overseeing her life and care for most of my life." Mother was totally uncooperative with Janet and verbally abused her at every turn.

We decided that Janet's husband, Joe, would accompany her on all visits to her mother's home. She would only take her mother out to eat if no alcohol was involved. The next time Mother felt the need for help, she was instructed to call 911 and be transported to the hospital. The hospital would then contact Janet. Janet decided to visit infrequently, with occasional phone contacts to gather a list of groceries that her mother needed. All these boundaries were put into place as Janet waited for the approval of guardianship. Because her mother refused to go look at alternative living options, Janet made the plans and later explained to her mother, as best she could, that this was for her own safety.

When the day came, Janet and her sister tearfully placed their mother in a place where she could be lovingly looked after and cared for. Mother now had the opportunity to make new choices regarding how she wanted to treat others, including Janet. Janet told me that had she not had the opportunity to walk through these difficult steps with a Christian counselor, a support system in her church, and friends in her workplace; the guilt she felt not only from being born but from having the responsibility for another's life seemed far too heavy a burden to carry. Christ saw her through as He promised. Janet's mother is currently sober, taking meds for her bipolar disorder, and making a few new acquaintances. Janet now has the freedom to visit her mother not because she must but because she realizes that all her life she only wanted her mother to acknowledge her. Today, that has slowly begun to occur.

## Treatment Strategies for Partners and Others

The extreme stress and trauma reactions you may be experiencing because of narcissistic abuse and relational trauma can cause you—the victim—to experience mental confusion, emotional reactiveness, defensive responses, memory impairment, sleep deprivation, exhaustion from the chronic adrenaline output, and to feel like the crazy one. Gaslighting behaviors (see Appendix) describe how the narcissist uses information the victim has shared to make her seem crazy. In addition, the narcissist tells everyone who will listen that he is the victim. He uses the victim's responses to his insidious abuse against them as a means of justifying to others his own victimization.[2]

Researchers are now describing a phenomenon in which the betrayed person is so overwhelmed by their inability to find the capacity to cope that they now struggle to define the nature of the original relationship. What was a haven in times of stress is now a source of immense danger.[3] So what do you do and where do you go to find comfort and security?

We respond to emotional and psychological trauma in one of two ways: we make desperate attempts to reconnect with our abusive partner, or we do the opposite, building emotional walls to defend our hearts from the painful rejection, lack of care, and the intense loneliness and isolation.

Post-Traumatic Stress Disorder (PTSD) manifests in many and various ways. When you are the betrayed partner and experience repeated wounds, whether emotional, verbal, physical, or sexual, you will most likely show signs of PTSD and what is called Narcissistic Victim Syndrome. As a victim-survivor, you will require the help of a trauma-trained psychotherapist to move through intense grief and begin your healing.

Though not complete, a listing of PTSD symptoms include increased feelings of anxiety that result in behaviors like hyper-vigilance; scanning of the environment looking for potential signs of danger or threat; paranoia; overwhelming terror; insomnia; inability to concentrate; agoraphobia; exaggerated startle reflex; avoiding reminders or conversations as well as not remembering all aspects (blocking); re-experiencing the event(s) through thoughts, memories, flashbacks, and nightmares; increasing distress over time that impacts all life areas to include self-care, work, or daily responsibilities; or even the inability to participate in other relationships.[4]

A connection with a narcissistic person on any level can ultimately result in trauma, regardless of the specific type of relationship, whether boss/employee, parent/child, sibling/sibling, friend/friend, or a spouse or primary love interest. The mental health community has for years primarily focused upon the needs of the abuser, since alcoholism, drug addiction, sex addiction, compulsive gambling, and other addictive behaviors are often involved.

Twelve Step Groups provided a source of support for these individuals as well as for the partners who were abused. Al-Anon, Codependency Anonymous, or Co-Sex Addiction meetings gave hope to victims and provided a safe place where they could share their stories of intense emotional pain. Abuse at the hand of narcissists seems to have increased in the past ten years, while victims and professionals in the field are finding they need much more help than was formerly recognized.

Family of origin dynamics often provide "the grist for the codependency mill" in our lives. Because individuals are often "looking for love, security, and safety in all the wrong places," they find themselves attracted to what's familiar, even if the other person presents differently at first. Enabling, detachment, and effective boundary setting skills are required to help partners heal.

Although we have touched on some of this information earlier in the text, it is worth repeating here so that if this applies to your personal situation, you will be affirmed that it is time to seek outside help and support for all that you are experiencing.

Current clients are reporting increasing incidences of sexual betrayal in their relationships and marriages. When this occurs, individuals lose what for them was the safest environment they knew previously—until they could no longer trust their partners. The result is that victims are left broken and separated from the very people with whom they feel their deepest attachment bonds.[5]

Deep understanding and empathy must be mirrored back to individuals who have experienced this type of trauma. If this has happened to you, it is imperative that you feel affirmed as a person of great worth and value. Believing there is great hope for the restoration of your own lives is imperative! The pain you have endured at the hand of the one you most loved, trusted, and often had a family and plans for a future and a hope with have now been shattered. The "heart of the matter—is the matter of the heart." And your heart has been ravaged, broken, and torn apart.

It becomes imperative to seek help for your own healing because it is likely that you have been enduring a chronic state of reactiveness to your own fight, flight, or freeze emotional response. Over time, having stress hormones flowing through your body in the form of adrenaline and cortisol can wear down normal tissue and set the victim up for multiple potential disease states. This is not a normal way to live.

When an abused partner begins to gain knowledge and strength to move forward in a way that reveals your desire to take better care of yourself, the narcissist will probably view this as an affront or assault to him. He may attempt to increase his level of control as he recognizes he may be losing control over you. What truly is happening is that as you slowly begin to act upon your own thoughts and feelings, the mechanisms the narcissist used to keep all things hidden begins to give way to the truth. Denial begins to erode, and you begin to regain your own voice that allows you to speak on your own behalf.

The following list includes steps that may be useful to consider as your primary goals in boundary skill development—identifying what you can and cannot live with any longer.

## Self-Care Program—How to Begin

**1. Surrender to the Lord in Prayer**—Draw closer to the Lord, and He will draw closer to you. Remember, this is a spiritual battle, so put on the full armor of God. The battle is not with flesh and blood, but with the spiritual forces of evil.[6] The outcome is not yours, so be strong in the Lord, and the Lord will fight for you. Surrender to Him and say, "Not my will, Lord, but Yours be done." Identify a spiritual mentor to walk this path with you.

**2. Psychotherapy**—Do a Google search for Christian therapists in your geographical area. The *Psychology Today* website allows you to search your city and state to identify trauma-trained therapists as well. Find a tough-minded, highly skilled, trauma-trained, compassionate Christian therapist who understands spiritual warfare, personality disorders, and the long-term effects of trauma on survivors. You may need to visit with a few before deciding upon the one who best fits your specific needs. Don't be afraid to ask them about their experience working with your issues before making a choice to work with them. Psychotherapy can help you gain knowledge and understanding regarding the reasons you have tolerated abuse, neglect, and betrayal in your relationship with the NPD person. Second, you need biblical guidance to learn how to walk through the process of healing to freedom. An experienced psychotherapist can help you design a biblically sound battle plan.

**3. Support Team**—Create a strong, caring, supportive team of people who understand the spiritual battle you are facing and the complexities of spiritual warfare. Draw close to those who will pray for and with you—like a small group, pastor, or Bible study group, along with safe family members and friends.

**4. Support Group**—If the NPD person in your life is involved in any addictive behaviors, seek out appropriate support groups such as Al-Anon, Codependency Anonymous, Co-Sex Addiction Groups, and Celebrate Recovery, a Christian-based, Twelve-Step Recovery Program often located in churches. Consider attending one of New Life Ministry's weekend programs like "Take Your Life Back" or "Restored." Information is available online at www.newlife.com.

**5. Seek Legal Support**—Compose a complete list of questions before your first appointment. Even if you do not know where your marriage is headed, you need legal support and advice. Select an attorney who is familiar with the behavioral strategies used by the NPD individual. You will need answers about how to secure an emotionally safe distance (inside the home or out); protect all financial assets, particularly if the narcissist is in control of the finances; and access medical and mental health services for

you and your children. Learn what your child custody rights are in
your state. Explore options regarding your rights to secure financial funding from credit cards, loans, family, or friends. Discuss
restraining orders where appropriate. Know how to access local
police, emergency squads, and Child Protective Services in your
area.

**6. Dealing with Emotional Stuckness**—As the process
unfolds, and you begin to break through your own denial, anger
and rage may surface and require expression. It is likely you will
need help addressing complex PTSD symptoms. As you move forward, forgiveness will be a part of the process, but now is not the
time to focus on forgiveness. First identify your own unresolved
resentments, bitterness, and regrets regarding how you enabled the
NPD's destructive behavior, regardless of whether you may even
understand that just yet.

**7. Consider How Changing Your Reactions Can Benefit
You**—Explore the following and ask for help to make changes:[7]

> A. Explore the patterns you've used to get your
> own needs met for love, affirmation, affection,
> recognition, safety, and security.
> B. Consider the ways you react to what others
> say, do, and think, especially when you don't feel
> safe, secure, or comfortable.
> C. Stop accepting criticism as personal. Although
> the NPD will blame and direct his anger toward
> you, practice telling yourself that his behavior is
> not about what you did, said, or how you acted.

See his accusations more as a mirror reflection of what he may be experiencing internally (although he is projecting it onto you).

D. Repeat yourself only enough to decide whether the narcissist has heard you yet chooses not to respond. Ask directly whether he heard you.

E. Improve your problem-solving skills. Stand firm in your own beliefs while taking the other person's side into consideration. Consider offering an alternative solution with a more balanced perspective that includes his ideas, too. Check with your support network before sharing with the NPD individual in your life.

F. Stay calm and make direct eye contact. Whether the narcissist turns away or not, speak slowly, clearly, and with a firm voice. Focus on your breathing so if anger, fear, or resentment surface, you will be able to continue.

**8. Learn Gentle Confrontation Skills**—If the situation and/or circumstances require some type of confrontation in the hope of a "breakthrough" with the NPD person, first seek assistance. There are many ways to proceed, but writing out all your thoughts is a good way to begin. When it's time to move forward toward reconciliation or an agreement to end the marriage, a separate and complete set of guidelines will need to be addressed.

**9. Practice Basic Steps of Self-Care**—Learn to say what you mean and mean what you say. Do not threaten. Do not be afraid to say "no" if something frightens you or you are uncomfortable with it. Trust your own instincts. Do not use negative self-talk, referring to yourself by names you have been called. Be kind to yourself, never shaming yourself for mistakes you have made. Do not give up. Instead, practice letting go of what you cannot control or change. Distance yourself from people who use drama, speak negatively, and talk badly about others. If you have not had a medical check-up for a time, see your primary care physician, especially if you and your therapist suspect symptoms of depression, anxiety, or you discover your partner's infidelity. Practice loving more by beginning with you!

Each one of you has different life experiences with someone you believe to be narcissistic. Although it would be impossible to address all possible combinations of scenarios, we've selected a few that we believe may be representative of a body of reported experiences. You may formulate questions or comments as you review. Write these in a journal as you proceed, then have them answered by the key people in your support network.

## Sample Scenarios of Narcissistic Interactions

**1. Mother with Adult Children**—Although Sheri's father is suffering with progressive Alzheimer's Disease, her focus has always been drawn away from her dad because of her mother's self-centered attitudes her whole life. Sheri and her siblings are now grown adults with families of their own. Rather than show compassion to her husband, Sheri's mother complains daily to anyone who will listen about how burdened her life has become since she has became her husband's primary caretaker. She uses every opportunity to sneak away with her friends, even if it means she lies to her children about how much time she leaves their dad alone. Sheri fully understands the responsibility of caring for someone with personal impairments since she is raising a special needs child of her own. Her mother, though, became emotionally reliant upon Sheri as her narcissistic supply early in life and now capitalizes on Sheri's attention because she doesn't want to burden her three sons!

**Response**—The siblings agreed it is time to relocate their dad to a safer emotional environment where his needs can be addressed. Their mother insists, however, she not be left out when anyone comes to visit their dad. Each sibling has expressed the desire for time alone with Dad since his remaining time is uncertain. Mother constantly interrupts, turning all conversations to her expressed needs or interests. She is demeaning and disrespectful in front of her husband, often speaking for him to her children and grandchildren.

A family meeting that included their mother was organized as soon as their dad's relocation was completed. Coaching helped Sheri learn how to define needed boundaries to deal with interruptions, talking over everyone present, saying hurtful things about their dad, and other approaches that could help secure ways for each family member to spend time alone with Dad. It was agreed in advance that the meeting would be stopped if these guidelines were not observed. It was suggested that each family member make separate plans with Mother to go out for meals or make time-limited visits at her home or at each of their own homes so that their mother would not be left out of their lives. Then they could focus on her without the competition she felt with her husband present. This, so far, has become a win-win!

**2. Brother and Adult Sister**—Jack's older sister has always been a painful source of irritation for him. At holiday gatherings, Joanie constantly uses Jack as her "scapegoat" by making disparaging remarks about his intelligence while bringing up the same embarrassing stories from the past. While both siblings are college graduates, Joanie teaches business classes in the local high school. Jack's career has progressed as a financial analyst with a prestigious Chicago firm. Jack has begun to avoid going home for family visits to avoid conflict with Joanie. On previous visits, he always stayed in her apartment. He wants change in their relationship.

**Response**—Jack was coached to get his thoughts and feelings down on paper before his next communication with Joanie. He was encouraged to outline his goals in a way that would potentially benefit both him and Joanie. Writing out a brief statement about what he hopes to achieve by addressing Joanie directly will help him be clear yet firm in his requests. These are the key points he chose to make:

"You are my older sister and I care for you; I plan to stay connected to you over time; I respect much about what you do and how successful you have been. However, I don't enjoy the conflict that occurs when I come for a family visit. From now on, if I hear any insults, criticism, or experience the instigation of any personal attacks, I will know that you are not in a place for me to be around you. If I had planned to stay with you, I will find a safe place to stay. I may ask you to sign a connection contract if this should continue to happen within the family."

Spelling out the consequences in advance for the narcissist allows them to have a choice in the matter while identifying what is expected for them to participate fully.

**3. Husband and Wife**—Sam was "the social butterfly" when Jodie married him. His need for many friends, an active social life, and a lot of time with his own family seemed a given. Jodie enjoyed getting to know his friends and family; however, she planned to maintain regular contact with her own long-time friends and family. Not long after they married, Jodie experienced Sam's derogatory comments when she tried to share her interests and experiences. Sam always made certain they visited his family and friends first at the holidays.

Jodie's closest girlfriend called their home number often. Sam complained he didn't really like her calling so frequently. He took Jodie by surprise when he expressed strongly, "I don't really think your friend even likes me!" Jodie couldn't believe what she was hearing since Sam had never even met the friend. He finally said he didn't want her calling the house nor did he want Jodie continuing to see her. By now, he'd begun complaining about the way her family treated her as well and said he thought she should stay away from them, too.

**Response**—Alienation is a form of emotional abuse. This can be as damaging as being denied one's physical needs for sleep and nutrition. No one has the right to deny access to who we see and where we go in loving, healthy relationships. If it becomes chronic, individuals can experience the classic stages of grief. Do not remain silent about what is happening. Get support from trusted others. Talk with the people from whom you are being isolated. Make up your own mind about the kind of people they are.

Directly confront any attempts to isolate you. Speak firmly and calmly. Tell your partner that you care a great deal for him; however, make it clear that you also care about your own health.

Seeing friends and family is something you need to do. Visit these others regularly by yourself, even if the narcissist insists you don't. If this is not enough, find a counselor who can help you clarify your situation and offer tips about how to set boundaries and consequences. Sam is unfair when he makes their plans to spend time with his select friends while criticizing friends he's never met, and this behavior leaves her feeling unimportant and invalidated. Jodie needs to inform him that she will continue to visit where and when it is appropriate for her, assuring him that their marriage relationship is her number one priority.

**4. A Young Engaged Couple**—Ben and Holly are a "thirty-something" engaged couple. They have been together all through graduate school and are both successfully employed in busy careers. No plans have yet been finalized for the wedding. They are heard justifying this fact by explaining to others that "Everything is always or never right!" Absolutes are expressions that leave little if any "wiggle room" for someone to get it right for the other. Holly frequently uses the words *always* and *never* when Ben doesn't agree with her. When she frames things this way, Ben feels he's being accused of something, an argument is brewing, or Holly is acting in a self-pitying way that really irritates him. If we listened in, we'd hear remarks like, "You never listen to anything I say to you!" "I always give you exactly what you want!" "I hate it when you always have to have the last word!" And then there's the "No matter what I do for you, I can never get your full attention!"

**Response**—Always and never statements are rarely used with the expectation that they will be taken literally. However, when used during intense conflict, the meaning is to invoke fear, obligation, and guilt in the other person. The recipient is put in a defensive posture, left feeling responsible for the problem, and is often left feeling invalidated, unappreciated, disoriented, and possibly guilty, somehow thinking they should have done it differently. Sadly, the purpose is rarely to establish objective truth. Generally, the goal is to provoke an emotional response or escalate a conflict already in process; as such, the real issue is rarely identified.

Do not make attempts to argue your case. Listen carefully to what is being said to see whether you can understand the feeling that is driving the process. Get a little distance by stating that you need time to process what's been shared to determine what part you can take ownership of. Find a supportive person to discuss this with, like a friend, pastor, or counselor. Look between the "black and white" of what is being presented to see any areas of gray. If the relationship becomes verbally abusive, remove yourself and any children within earshot. In a quiet time, it might be important to share with the other person how these kinds of accusations box you in, making it impossible for you to help either of them get what they want and need.

**5. Therapist and Client**—John is Karen's client at the VA Center. When I talked with Karen about her work with John, this is what she told me: "John is a guy who is generally derogatory and belittling, leaving everyone around him with the feeling that he is owed something, and they're just holding back, unwilling to give him what he wants. He is hypercritical and harassing when he doesn't get his way." Karen believes John's early life included a history of poverty and abuse. She's clear that rigid gender roles were adhered to, so John never felt he could ever express any vulnerability publicly. Karen described that despite her professional belief that there is hope for every client, she has also learned in the process that clinicians must learn to protect themselves from being beaten down or taken advantage of in the process of aiding another with their life problems. Recognizing our own personal/professional limits is imperative, even when it requires us to be vulnerable in the process.

**Response**—Karen's response was to immediately establish tighter boundaries in working with demanding clients like John. She decides how and when he speaks with her and under what circumstances. She becomes focused and assertive in expressing exactly the kinds of help she can provide and identifying the acceptable manner she is willing to talk with John. She speaks to him with great respect; however, when he begins to belittle her, she does not hesitate to cut their time together short, distancing herself from his abusive words and actions. Karen points out her unwillingness to volley back and forth, as John attempts to break her down. She chooses to stand firm on what she feels certain she can provide and does not concede under pressure.

The outcome in John's case was that as Karen stood firm, John decided to climb "the food chain." He called for a supervisor who respectfully supported the actions Karen had taken while removing the client from the program currently offered to him. John was placed in a lower-intensity program, one that required less of him. Karen realized, as she let go of the belief that the client's response was a primary indicator of her worth as a social worker, that she could move on while choosing to discontinue all contact with him. Her goal had been to treat John with respect and dignity regardless of his actions toward her. In the end, she chose to believe that in doing God's work, we may only be the one who plants the seeds, turning over the right to know in this lifetime whether we ever make a difference. However, it may be equally important to let others know that their unwarranted behaviors may carry life consequences. That, too, may be part and parcel of seed planting.

Even though Karen's scenario was identified as a professional with a very narcissistic client, the tight boundaries Karen set brought about exactly what the client needed for the level of personal involvement he was willing to invest. Karen's attitude clearly reinforces the fact that if someone else does not want what we have to offer, we may need to cut our losses and move on. We also must make certain not to carry the burden of the other's plight in life. And finally, we must maintain hope above all else. Without God's Holy Spirit working in and through our lives, that would be almost impossible to do during trying circumstances. We must hold firmly to the promise that "when I am weak, He is strong."

We've looked at a few examples of ways to interact with the narcissist in your life. What you choose to do and how you do it depends upon your relationship. If the narcissist is an adult son rather than a boss or leader you work with, the options will vary. As we move forward, let's take a closer look at what to do when nothing you try seems to bring about change in the narcissist.

The Appendix includes a complete list of the most damaging and destructive behaviors used by narcissists. Additional scenarios can also be found there regarding how to approach and deal with a variety of these harmful behaviors.

# CHAPTER 7

# What to Do When What You've Tried Isn't Working

Come to me, all you who are weary and burdened, and I will give you rest.

—Matthew 11:28[1]

It was through the storms of life that the disciples learned who Jesus really was, what He could do, and what their own potential was. I suspect by now, you may be weary and feeling heavily burdened in your personal relationship with the narcissist in your life. As believers, we need to remind ourselves that nothing is random in the Lord's kingdom. Jesus says, "to those who love Me," everything fits into a pattern for good. He promises us that nothing is wasted when we walk close to Him daily. Even our own mistakes and sins can be recycled into something good. And this happens not in our strength; it happens by God's transforming grace.

If you have reached this chapter, it's clear that you have related to many of the examples given, and you have learned from what you have heard. I might guess that you may even have tried some of the suggestions already offered within the text.

However, I believe some of you—maybe many of you—believe that you still need more. You want to save your marriage because you're not ready to give up—or you can't imagine losing a connection with an adult son or daughter. Possibly, leaving your employment with a boss who fits the description of a narcissist is just not an option yet! Don't stop reading. There is more to consider here.

David Smith is the Senior Pastor at Fairhaven Church in Dayton, Ohio. He recently preached a message, and what stuck out for me were these few important words: "Jesus doesn't make a better version of you. He makes a whole new version of you." Pastor David went on to say that "Jesus is better experienced than explained" and that "our fleshly cravings are satisfied when we find our satisfaction in Jesus."[2] Too many times, we look for fulfillment in our relationship with another person. A common expression in the mental health field is this, "Codependent people don't make friends, they take hostages!"

If you've read this far, I want to remind you of this: "The Lord is close to the brokenhearted and saves those who are crushed in spirit."[3] God wants to be our guide, especially in circumstances as difficult as being in relationship with a narcissistic person. Sometimes, when it seems that all is not working, we must wait on the Lord. Not easy to do, I know! We often want to run ahead, doing things our own way, trying to relieve the pain, shame, hurt, fear, or loneliness. Although I have said this earlier, if you and your children are in any kind of danger, it is wise to remove yourselves—with the help of supportive others—to a safe location. Always keep this in mind as we go forward.

It's important to do our own personal tune-ups to see whether we are running on empty. Ask yourself first whether you are willing to do and try everything that is suggested. God often asks us to commit to His way—even before we know what's going to happen. I remember clearly in my own marriage of more than thirty-three years, when the pain I felt was so excruciating that I couldn't imagine how I could go on, I got down on my knees and sobbed, saying to the Lord, "I will do anything You ask me to do. I will go through this pain and more if You will change my heart and carry me through to the other side."

My journey was a faith walk because I didn't see any changes coming from my spouse. The closer I drew to the Lord, the relationship between my husband and myself deteriorated. He shut me out even more, stonewalling in tense silence until one of us needed something from the other.

God calls us all to have a teachable spirit, a tender heart, and a surrendered will. When people hurt us badly, we want to strike out, but the Lord says that vengeance is His and His alone. Our part is to live at peace with everyone. His reminder to us is, "Do not be overcome by evil, but overcome evil with good."[4] Relationships with narcissistic people can make us feel like we're doing battle with the devil every day. Draw close to the Lord, and He will draw close to you.

Remember Tori and Kevin's story? Tori saw the movie *War Room* shortly before things escalated in her marriage with Kevin. Kevin was determined to continue his pattern of infidelity—and by now Tori had prayed to let go of her need to control Kevin's behavior. She shared with me that she spent quiet time with the Lord daily in the private space she created in her home. Just as

Jesus needed to get away from the crowds to spend time with His Father, we need to lean into Him and listen for His responses to our prayers and our situations, which often can only be heard in a gentle whisper, "a still, small voice."

## The Secret to Victorious Living

When all your attempts to improve your relationship with the narcissist in your life haven't worked, consider some of the following suggestions:

1. Focus on God's presence in your life. If you are a believer, you are a child of God. Therefore, He is as close to you as your own breath. Talk with Him when no one else will acknowledge you.

2. Transfer your emotional dependency from the NPD person in your life to God. Every moment, remind yourself that "I can do all this through him who gives me strength" (Philippians 4:13). If the narcissist cannot meet your needs for connection and companionship, rely on God's Word.

3. Unless the Spirit moves you, God's message is often to "stay where you are," unless physical, emotional, and sexual safety are at risk for you or your children. Collaborate with your support network on every project, task, or mountain you must climb, praying in the Spirit on all occasions (Ephesians 6:18).

4. Acknowledge that the problem in all of us is the "sin which dwells in me."[5] The enemy tempts us toward words, actions, attitudes, and behaviors that are unkind, retaliatory, and vengeful. He knows we're weak, vulnerable, and exhausted. If you fall, repent quickly—change your thinking, go in a different direction, move toward God and not away.

5. Pray constantly on behalf of those who refuse to believe that Jesus offered Himself, "once for all" to make atonement with the Father for the sins of the past, present, and future.[6] Pray for the NPD person to accept God's precious gift of forgiveness and life eternal.

6. Make amends to those you have harmed by not loving them well. Even though we may have done the best we could at the time, we can always apologize and/or change the way we interact with others. Even when our hearts have been wounded and damaged by the narcissist's insults, attacks, betrayals, and rejection, we can make the effort to own any contribution we might have added that made life stressful for them.

7. Stop trying to please, measure up, and seek approval from the NPD person. Working to receive validation from someone who makes you feel bad or not "good enough" only sets you up to feel more defensive, struggling to do things perfectly, even work harder to feel good about yourself. If you find that you can't shake the feeling of disapproval and disappointment, step back. When you believe the narcissist's insults, self-doubt and negative self-talk sets in. This is a crippling way to live. Throw off those shackles by connecting with loving, caring, supportive people. Rebuke the enemy with powerful scriptural verses. Read Henry Cloud and John Townsend's book on *Safe People*.

8. You may find that the "critical judge" in your head is left over from your formative years in a household with a controlling parent, teacher, older sibling, or even a bully on the playground. Recognize that the NPD person in your life can hook into those negative thoughts about yourself more easily than you know. Be cautious not to play defensive catch-up. Address these issues with

the help of an expert. It does a body good to learn the art of positive self-talk.

9. If you are enabling the narcissist by standing in the gap for him with other people, it's time to stop! He uses the positive feelings or energy he gets when you talk about his affairs, addictions, awards, accolades, and acquisitions of people and things in an attempt to soothe his own aching soul. Take a step back and evaluate your own actions. This concept of enabling is so incredibly important at this point in your healing—and frankly, it's imperative that you consider the following suggestions so that you may be able to maintain hope for the healing of the narcissist:

- Helping him shift blame onto others instead of you.
- Flattering him with dishonest appraisals about his performance or the ways he operates with others.
- Agreeing with the NPD's controlling decisions that involve you even when you know they aren't right for you.
- Continuing to tell yourself that he can do no wrong when he is demonstrating the opposite.

Detachment means learning how to identify and let go of things that are not good for your own life, growth, and health. We need relationships like we need air, water, and food. Sometimes, we hold onto the pain in the relationship with the NPD person because we, too, fear experiencing our own vulnerability. We need to acknowledge that we truly need more people in our lives than just the NPD person to thrive and grow.

When Ella, one of the clients from our earlier stories, was born, she experienced significant birth trauma, which required emergency intervention, followed by multiple complete blood transfusions. Ella was repeatedly reminded about that time in her early life, but never in a manner that left her feeling good about herself. The messages imprinted in her mind were often the hurtful things her narcissistic, alcoholic father spoke aloud while reminding her that she was different, she didn't fit in with the rest of the family, "There must be something wrong with you," and, finally, the most hurtful words: "You don't belong in this family."

By the time she had reached adulthood, Ella had unknowingly learned to pick relationships that would reenact the same scenario. She would pick relationships that would validate her feelings of low self-worth. When she met and married Richard, not having any idea of his narcissistic personality, she married into a blended family. Her husband constantly reminded her that she couldn't stepparent his family well enough to suit him or his children. It wasn't until the pain and shame projected on her because of Richard's own failings as a father and husband twice before began to squeeze the life right out of her that she became willing and open to any way that would help her through the pain. God plucked Ella out of the depths of the dark hole of pain that had grown so deep she couldn't see how to climb out. Then people came into her life to help her see that God loved her no matter how Richard and his children treated her. And that if she would invite Jesus into her heart, He alone would forgive her sins forever and love her with an amazing grace-filled love.

One day, while following her husband in her own car, she heard God speak to her heart. In only a few short words, she heard, "Follow him—or follow Me!" Ella was so astounded that she hungered to learn more about this God who was close enough to speak to her … and she could hear Him. It was the beginning of Ella knowing the right thing to do. Detachment from what she had tried so hard to change on her own—Richard and his confusing, dishonest ways— was not only futile; it was dangerous. At times, through many years, suicide had seemed her only way out.

Today Ella describes her experience as the "divine reversal." The God who had saved her life right after birth with blood transfusions was now working to bring about a total transformation in her life by accepting Christ's blood sacrifice on the cross and His forgiveness for her sins. Making the final choice to leave Richard came in a flash after he pointedly told her, "I divorce you in the eyes of God!" What her husband had said, intending to crush her spirit, was enough for Ella to know it was time to save her own life by putting space between herself and Richard.

It wasn't until Ella had found some safety in the "no contact" guideline and her heart was slowly beginning to heal that she realized how very much she truly loved this man who could not love her well. Theirs was an immature love, the kind that brought aching and hurt to their hearts daily. By this time, Richard had serious heart issues, yet by God's grace in one private moment after their divorce was finalized, Richard told Ella, "You were truly the only love of my life." Even though he could not embrace that love or live it out in a way that was evident to Ella, she knew God had softened her heart to once again feel the great sadness of another life gone wrong. Richard died almost three years to the day of their divorce—at home ... alone. It was an amazingly sad day for all who loved him, including Ella.

## Additional Strategies to Consider When Dealing with a Narcissist You Love

**Check Your Partner's Willingness to Change**—Actions speak louder than words. You must risk asking your partner whether he is willing to jointly see a counselor and attend any kind of healing intervention program to address co-occurring disorders like infidelity, drug addiction, or alcoholism. If the answer is yes, be willing to make the arrangements and follow up. If the narcissist in your life refuses, back away and focus your energy on your own healing. If he agrees to see a counselor and quits after a session or two, saying, "This really isn't working for me," back away.

**Check Your Anger at the Door**—Let's face it, when your partner sneers at you and tells you how jealous you are for always checking up on him, it's challenging not to unload your anger and engage with a statement like, "You're the most selfish, self-centered person I know—and look who's calling who jealous!"

Instead, risk being vulnerable one more time by saying something like, "You mean so much to me," or "Our marriage is so important to me that when you don't tell me who you're talking with on the phone and I hear those conversations, I get scared that I'm not enough for you. I value your opinion, and when you talk to me in a way that leaves me feeling small and worthless, I feel that distance growing between us—and that frightens me."

Anger is the emotion that seems to cover all others. When we can risk sharing our sadness and fear beneath the anger, it is worth the chance that the more vulnerable narcissist may be able to relate to you.

**Check for Denial**—It's important to check for denial in your partner or adolescent child. It's a powerful yet common defense mechanism. An alcoholic may say he drinks because he truly likes the taste of wine. If you're dealing with an adolescent in denial, it is an important predictor of the future development of both ruthless and demanding narcissistic behavior. Ask simple questions that will prompt a narcissistic person to admit or acknowledge that something's wrong—even if only to say, "My life is not where I'd hoped it would be."

Some narcissists do seek therapy, even on their own, particularly if they recognize they are riddled with shame and fear that results in both depression and anxiety. Those who dare to ask for help are the more vulnerable or covert narcissists. If they can admit to themselves that they do have some problems, there is great hope. But if they continue in denial and blame you for everything, saying you're the problem and their lives would be great if you'd fix your own issues, then focus on your own healing.

**Check Your Own Use of Silence**—You've heard me mention earlier that silence is one of the most abusive things a couple can do to each other. I'm not talking about the kind of silence needed to think over and process something internally. I'm talking about the kind of silence that shuts partners out. When the narcissist says something that feels hurtful to you, it's possible to risk asking him what he really means. You can tell him that you don't want to jump to conclusions; then you can ask if he would be willing to help explain what he just said.

If your typical method of operating is to slink away because your self-esteem has just taken a hit, risk trying something new. Stand firm in the moment and express what you're experiencing that previously would have sent you packing to hide out—away from your partner. Tell him, "I'm feeling so put down right now that I'm afraid when you say those hurtful things to me that you don't really care about me anymore," or "Is that what you're really saying to me? Because if it is, I need to know where I stand with you."

Consider that if you believe you're at your limit when you become angry or withdraw from him, your actions will likely ramp up the narcissist's insecurities. In retaliation, he will come back with his primary defenses to protect himself—like using more criticism, indifference, contempt, or a host of other hurtful defenses. This is his narcissism. (See Appendix for a listing of most hurtful behaviors.)

**Be Honest with Yourself**—Narcissistic arrogance and hostility get under our skin and bring out the worst behaviors in us. The natural response to this kind of behavior, whether in the workplace, our relationships, or with family, is to pull away or lash back. This behavior confirms what the narcissist believes internally about himself, even though he's unable to own the role his behavior plays in these scenarios.

If you don't share your pain in a softer way, you'll never know whether he can truly hear you or not. You may only get one more shot, but you've got to try it so you'll know what's possible. If you try to communicate and he can't understand your pain, perhaps he never will. As sad as this is, this is what you are trying to find out. Can he change? Is he willing to try to change for the sake of your relationship? Regardless of what tactic, strategy, diversion, or habit the narcissist uses to avoid genuine love and intimacy with you, if he refuses to change, then his problems are here to stay. If you continue in the relationship, his problems will remain yours, too!

**Check for Abuse**—If any kind of abuse is going on, then the suggestions given above are not likely to be of any help. Although it seems to be reported rarely, not all NPDs are abusive. It doesn't matter much what the reasons are for the abuse—whether chronic pain, alcoholism, or drug addiction—the abuser is fully responsible for his choice to abuse. Unless his behavior changes, it's unlikely you will feel safe enough to try some of the risk-taking strategies suggested here—even as a last-ditch effort.

**Focus on the Facts, Not on Your Emotions**—Our minds play tricks on us when it comes to what's true. Feelings often lie. For example, if the narcissist tells you that you've failed at something, you jump to believing "I am a failure." It's healthy to express your thoughts and feelings with a safe support person. But in the process, seek the truth, trust the facts, and remember, "It's the truth that sets us free."

**Check Yourself to See If You Are Making Comparisons**— Don't compare yourself or your circumstances with others. This thinking always weakens us, leaving us more vulnerable to the downward spiral of negative thinking and self-talk. We start telling ourselves that we're not good enough and never will be. We compare our feelings with the outside mask of the narcissist. He tells you that you're less than you are because at some level he is feeling that about himself. Did you ever consider that despite what he says to you, he's watching how you live your life? He may be measuring his life against yours. Let go of self-criticism.

**Be Cautious about Accepting False Blame**—Just because everything you've tried with the narcissist in your life hasn't worked, do not accept responsibility for his or her choice to stay the same. This burden is too heavy. We are not responsible for another person's responses. The most we can hope to achieve is to influence the narcissist, recognizing that we can't change him.

**Don't Exaggerate the Negative**—Sometimes others threaten us because they recognize the influence we have over others. The covert narcissist secretly loathes any good fortune or positive qualities you may have, so they work to make you out to be the fool or coward. They also threaten you to make you stop what you're doing. This happens often in workplaces where a higher pay grade person sets you up to publicly fall flat on your face to tarnish your good works with others.

**Take Care of Your Physical Needs**—Eat balanced meals, drink plenty of water, incorporate exercise or movement into your life several times weekly, and get plenty of rest. Chances are you've been running on a hamster wheel for a long time. It's okay to step off.

**Get Your Focus Off You and the Narcissist for a Time**—Before now, you haven't had the ability to focus on anything but your relationship with the narcissist. Slowly, consider adding one small new direction to your life. Look at those around you who also need support and help. As God continues to pour into your life, His expectation is simply that we will use what He has given us to help others.

**Evaluate Your Thinking for Irrational Thoughts**—With the help of a trusted friend, counselor, or pastor, look at whether you are holding onto some irrational thoughts. They become strongholds that keep us stuck. In Alcoholics Anonymous, they call it *stinkin' thinkin'*. Here's a few examples:

- If someone criticizes, judges, or discounts me, it means I'm worthless.
- I must be loved and accepted by everyone to feel fulfilled or "good enough" about myself and my life.
- I can't admit any areas of weakness I may have because I must be perfect at all things or others will see me as a failure.

Without the power of Christ living in our innermost being, we do not have the power to even change ourselves. How can we expect the wounded individual with all the symptoms, qualities, and characteristics of NPD to have the power needed to change—without Christ in him? It may be just the time for us to turn our lives over to Him—and surrender!

# CHAPTER 8

# Surrender—Not My Will, Lord, but Yours Be Done

Be strong and courageous. Do not be afraid; do not be discouraged, for the LORD your God will be with you wherever you go.

—Joshua 1:9[1]

The most significant question everyone asks when they discover they're in any type of relationship with a narcissistic person, whether a partner or spouse, a relative, an adult child, a friend, a coworker, or a boss, is "Will they ever change?" Research has taught us recently that the answer is a definite "maybe." Yet the real question being asked here tugs at our hearts and souls. That question is "*Can* the narcissist ever change?" Researchers and therapists, along with partners of narcissists, say that "change is possible—and guaranteed; it takes a great deal of work on the part of both parties in the relationship!"[2]

Current literature implies that *some* narcissists are generally quite successful, possessing a measure of healthy self-esteem, while they seem genuinely confident about who they are and what they do. They are the most common type of narcissist—extroverted, and most often pursuing power and attention.[3] We know that a few have made significant contributions in the world. Most of these types we might find more readily in the halls of celebrities. Some would identify Donald Trump to have a narcissistic profile, and it seems that as a business tycoon, he has been very successful. We also know that those with full-blown clinical NPD are the most vulnerable and dangerous, more easily threatened with a strong sense of entitlement. Sensitive to even the slightest hint of criticism, they may become emotionally out of control, regardless of the damage and destruction they leave behind.

If this is a romantic relationship, you may have invested your whole heart only to discover that where the balance differentials vary is in the realm of emotional investment. If you find that he is unwilling to listen to you and to hear your thoughts and feelings, particularly when a life change or adjustment is necessary, and his only response is to ask how it will affect him—this is a significant red flag. Narcissists lack compassion. Some narcissists cannot put the needs of an ill family member or child before their own personal needs, often complaining about the inconvenience they present because they are sick. At times, an NPD person will totally abandon and neglect the impaired person.

It is imperative that primary relationships include an element of empathy and compassion for them to thrive. Lack of empathy is a hallmark characteristic of most narcissists. Empathy refers to the capacity to experience life not just from our point of view but also from that of others, to feel the joy and sorrow of other people and to care about their well-being. Specialists in moral development consider empathy to be the foundation for human compassion and morality.[4] Researchers indicate that a complete lack of empathy marks a psychopathic personality.[5] It is the primary reason given to support how it is that narcissists have difficulty loving while some seem unable to love at all. Some therapists have reported that when the pressures that cause narcissists to be least empathic are not present for a time, they seem to be able to connect with a partner or other people for a brief time.[6]

The Lord's greatest command to us is to "love the Lord your God with all your heart, soul, mind, and strength."[7] After this, it is to love one another. When we have not learned to love well, it is immensely difficult to love one another. The wounded narcissist will project his problems on another person, which will serve only to break down that individual into less than the perfect image of who God destined him or her to become.

Loving another person under these conditions looks and feels very different from the kind of loving our hearts most desire. This loving requires our respect of the other. None with affliction are without some strengths, talents, and goodness. We must choose to respect that which is good and honorable in every person.

We choose to be compassionate, and within a compassionate heart is one who empathizes with the brokenness within the other. We have experienced what the narcissist is going through because he most often projects that very thing onto us! Almost fearful that we may try to comfort him, in his own deep-seated self-loathing, he pushes us even further away. The more truth we express or represent before him, the greater he must defend against it. Consider the following example:

Although Molly's story was not identified in detail previously, in a quiet moment before their final separation as they moved toward divorce, Molly asked Sam to come sit next to her on the sofa. Sam hesitatingly moved closer, although his discomfort was apparent. God had spoken to Molly's heart, asking her to risk one more time trying to comfort and connect with Sam. In her own fear of rejection, she asked Sam to lay his head in her lap while she proceeded to stroke his head and face. Few words were shared. After a brief time, Sam sat up, sheepishly looked at Molly, and said, "I know I should feel something for you after all these years, but honestly, I feel nothing." Molly followed God's lead and took a risk—although it didn't play out the way she had hoped—she knew that divorce was imminent from the man she loved. But …

Do we dare stop loving him who pushes us away and tries to make us look the fool? No, says the Gospel. In our own strength, we can do nothing. But with the help of the Lord, we can pray for the strength, courage, willingness, and mindfulness to continue to pray for the NPD person.[8]

*"Clothe yourselves with compassion, kindness, humility, gentleness and patience. Bear with each other and forgive one another if any of you has a grievance against someone. Forgive as the Lord forgave you. And over all these virtues put on love, which binds them all together in perfect unity."*[9]

This kind of love is about pleasing God, not people. For it is God who tests our hearts.[10] When living with someone whose brokenness becomes hurtful to the point of being toxic, it may be time to take steps to move forward with your own life. Speaking the truth in love is necessary … and "after you have suffered a little while," it is time, with help, to move on.[11]

Setting the necessary boundaries is, indeed, a loving act for yourself and the other person. Having a solid plan is essential. This will require the help and support of many others: therapist, pastor, small group, attorney, family, and friends. Your plan will include finding a suitable space for emotional safety within which you can focus on your own healing. If you have experienced symptoms of Post-Traumatic Stress Disorder, it is imperative that you seek counseling from a professionally trained trauma therapist. If medication is suggested and prescribed, be open and willing to accept it as necessary.

If children are involved, counseling may also be beneficial for them during this transitional phase. The person with NPD may love his children dearly and may not intentionally want to harm them. However, it is important to be aware that at times when the narcissist is short on his supply, especially during times of transition, it is possible that he might turn to one of the children to gain a measure of narcissistic supply. This can be damaging for the child regardless of the age or status.

After you have done all these things, stand firm, trusting the Lord God to lead, guide, protect, and provide for you in ways you cannot know or imagine.[12] We all ask ourselves the question, "How will I know if it's the right time to go?" "We cannot tolerate sin and go our own way in one area and expect to receive God's guidance in another. Sin will always mislead us. When your decision is unclear, ask yourselves these questions: Will Christ be glorified in this choice? Can I do this in Jesus' name?"[13]

Understand that getting out is *not* giving up! I had to learn that I could love the person without accepting or even tolerating destructive, hurtful, damaging behaviors—especially after I had made efforts to request that these cease. Continuing to live in this environment can cause the breakdown of one's entire being emotionally, physically, sexually, and spiritually. The choice to value one's own life more than the other is imperative—or you may lose your own life altogether!

Praying for the narcissistic person, regardless of your need to separate yourself from his damaging and destructive behaviors and actions, is something we are commanded to do as believers. Here are a few helpful Scriptures: Colossians 3:5, 8, 12, and 15. Jesus prayed for those who persecuted Him, and on the cross, He cried out to the Father, "Forgive them, for they do not know what they are doing."[14] Finally, Jesus says, "But to you who are listening I say: Love your enemies, do good to those who hate you, bless those who curse you, pray for those who mistreat you."[15]

"God, the Light of the world, is forever trying to get fallen humanity to alter their course. Arrogant humans who have chosen to 'captain' their own lives, usually charge on to their own destruction."[16] Dutch Sheets points to the discovery he made when identifying that more men are filled with prideful arrogance than are women. "After the fall, the desire to lead became the desire to dominate, or lord over; a giving nature turned into a getting nature; and a secure humility turned into an insecure pride"—possibly the root of what today appears as narcissism.[17]

## A Final Word

Marie was a young woman who was wooed by the pastor of a small southern Baptist church until she agreed to marry him. She knew little of his previous infidelity and earlier bouts with alcoholism. Twelve years her senior, John was looking for a narcissistic supply to meet his needs. Despite his broken promises to discontinue the infidelity, Marie put distance between them. She sought counseling and learned the necessity for firm boundaries if she chose to ever return to the marriage.

When John was suddenly diagnosed with cancer, Marie made the difficult but compassionate decision to aid him through his illness. During those long days, Marie was painfully honest with John about the hurt his abuse and betrayal had caused her. She challenged him to take ownership of his actions, which he was never able to do, pridefully contending that he'd done nothing wrong. Marie clung to her faith in God's steadfast promises that He alone would carry her through, no matter what that looked like. In the end, Marie kept her marriage vows … "Until death do us part." John passed away with Marie by his side.

Consider for a moment that the divine work God may be doing in and through your relationship with the narcissistic person in your life may be more about the transformation the cross is meant to bring about through your own life. All along, perhaps the "divine reversal" has been for you!

# Appendix

## Primary Destructive Behaviors and Mechanisms Used by Personality Disordered People, Including Narcissists

**Abusive Cycle**—The ongoing rotation between destructive and constructive behavior that is typical of many dysfunctional relationships and families.

**Alienation**—The act of cutting off or interfering with an individual's relationships with others.

**"Always" and "Never" Statements**—Declarations containing the words *always* or *never* are commonly used but rarely true.

**Anger**—People who suffer from personality disorders often feel a sense of unresolved anger and a heightened or exaggerated perception that they have been wronged, invalidated, neglected, or abused.

**Baiting**—A provocative act used to solicit an angry, aggressive, or emotional response from another individual.

**Belittling, Condescending, and Patronizing**—This kind of speech is a passive-aggressive approach to giving someone a verbal put-down while maintaining a facade of reasonableness or friendliness.

**Blaming**—The practice of identifying a person or people responsible for creating a problem rather than identifying ways of dealing with the problem.

**Bullying**—Any systematic action of hurting a person from a position of relative physical, social, economic, or emotional strength.

**Cheating**—Sharing a romantic or intimate relationship with somebody when you are already committed to a monogamous relationship with someone else.

**Chronic Broken Promises**—Repeatedly making and then breaking commitments and promises is a common trait among people who suffer from personality disorders.

**Denial**—Believing or imagining that some painful or traumatic circumstance, event, or memory does not exist or did not happen.

**Dissociation**—A psychological term used to describe a mental departure from reality.

**Domestic Theft**—Consuming or taking control of a resource or asset belonging to (or shared with) a family member, partner, or spouse without first obtaining their approval.

**Emotional Abuse**—Any pattern of behavior directed at one individual by another, which promotes in them a destructive sense of fear, obligation, or guilt (FOG).

**Emotional Blackmail**—A system of threats and punishments used to control someone's behaviors.

**False Accusations**—Patterns of unwarranted or exaggerated criticism directed toward someone else.

**Favoritism and Scapegoating**—Systematically giving a dysfunctional amount of preferential positive or negative treatment to one individual among a family group of peers.

**Frivolous Litigation**—The use of unmerited legal proceedings to hurt, harass, or gain an economic advantage over an individual or organization.

**Gaslighting**—The practice of brainwashing or convincing a mentally healthy individual that they are going insane or that their understanding of reality is mistaken or false. The term "Gaslighting" is based on the 1944 MGM movie *Gaslight*.

**Grooming**—Grooming is the predatory act of maneuvering another individual into a position that makes them isolated, dependent, trusting, and more vulnerable to abusive behavior.

**Harassment**—Any sustained or chronic pattern of unwelcome behavior by one individual toward another.

**Hoovers and Hoovering**—A Hoover is a metaphor taken from the popular brand of vacuum cleaners to describe how an abuse victim trying to assert their own rights by leaving or limiting contact in a dysfunctional relationship gets "sucked back in" when the perpetrator temporarily exhibits improved or desirable behavior.

**Imposed Isolation**—When abuse results in a person becoming isolated from their support network, including friends and family.

**Impulsiveness**—The tendency to act or speak based on current feelings rather than logical reasoning.

**Intimidation**—Any form of veiled, hidden, indirect, or nonverbal threat.

**Invalidation**—The creation or promotion of an environment that encourages an individual to believe that their thoughts, beliefs, values, or physical presence are inferior, flawed, problematic, or worthless.

**Lack of Conscience**—Individuals who suffer from personality disorders (PD) are often preoccupied with their own agendas, sometimes to the exclusion of the needs and concerns of others. This is sometimes interpreted as a lack of moral conscience.

**Low Self-Esteem**—A common name for a negatively distorted self-view.

**Manipulation**—The practice of steering an individual into a desired behavior to achieve a hidden personal goal.

**Masking**—Covering up one's own natural outward appearance, mannerisms, and speech in dramatic and inconsistent ways depending on the situation.

**Narcissism**—A set of behaviors characterized by a pattern of grandiosity, self-centered focus, need for admiration, self-serving attitude, and a lack of empathy or consideration for others.

**Neglect**—A passive form of abuse in which the physical or emotional needs of a dependent are disregarded or ignored by the person responsible for them.

**Normalizing**—Normalizing is a tactic used to desensitize an individual to abusive, coercive, or inappropriate behaviors. It is the manipulation of another human being to get them to agree to or to accept something that conflicts with the law, social norms, or their own basic code of behavior.

**"Not My Fault" Syndrome**—The practice of avoiding personal responsibility for one's own words and actions.

**No-Win Scenarios**—When you are manipulated into choosing between two bad options.

**Objectification**—The practice of treating a person or a group of people like an object.

**Parental Alienation Syndrome**—When a separated parent convinces their child that the other parent is bad, evil, or worthless.

**Pathological Lying**—Persistent deception by an individual to serve their own interests and needs with little or no regard to the needs and concerns of others. A pathological liar is a person who habitually lies to serve their own needs.

**Proxy Recruitment**—A way of controlling or abusing another person by manipulating other people into unwittingly "doing the dirty work."

**Raging, Violence, and Impulsive Aggression**—Explosive verbal, physical, or emotional elevations of a dispute. Rages threaten the security or safety of another individual and violate their personal boundaries.

**Ranking and Comparing**—Drawing unnecessary and inappropriate comparisons between individuals or groups.

**Relationship Hyper-Vigilance**—Maintaining an unhealthy level of interest in the behaviors, comments, thoughts, and interests of others.

**Sabotage**—The spontaneous disruption of calm or the status quo in order to serve a personal interest, provoke a conflict, or draw attention.

**Scapegoating**—Singling out one child, employee, or member of a group of peers for unmerited negative treatment or blame.

**Selective Memory and Selective Amnesia**—The use of memory, or a lack of memory, which is selective to the point of reinforcing a bias, belief, or desired outcome.

**Self-Aggrandizement**—A pattern of pompous behavior, boasting, narcissism, or competitiveness designed to create an appearance of superiority.

**Sense of Entitlement**—An unrealistic, unmerited, or inappropriate expectation of favorable living conditions and favorable treatment at the hands of others.

**Sexual Objectification**—Viewing another individual in terms of their sexual usefulness or attractiveness rather than pursuing or engaging in a quality interpersonal relationship with them.

**Shaming**—The difference between blaming and shaming is that in blaming someone tells you that you did something bad; in shaming, someone tells you that *you* are something bad.

**Stalking**—Any pervasive and unwelcome pattern of pursuing contact with another individual.

**Targeted Humor, Mocking, and Sarcasm**—Any sustained pattern of joking, sarcasm, or mockery designed to reduce another individual's reputation in their own eyes or in the eyes of others.

**Testing**—Repeatedly forcing another individual to demonstrate or prove their love or commitment to a relationship.

**Thought Policing**—Any process of trying to question, control, or unduly influence another person's thoughts or feelings.

**Threats**—Inappropriate, intentional warnings of destructive actions or consequences.

**Triangulation**—Gaining an advantage over perceived rivals by manipulating them into conflicts with each other.

**RESOURCE: www.outofthefog.com**

## Movies Portraying Narcissistic Personality Disorder Traits

**A Streetcar Named Desire**—*A Streetcar Named Desire* is a 1947 play written by Tennessee Williams, later adapted for film, which tells the story of a woman who displays histrionic and borderline traits, who goes to live with her codependent sister and her narcissistic husband.

**Black Swan**—*Black Swan* is a 2010 psychological thriller about a ballet dancer, played by Natalie Portman, who discovers a dark side to herself as she struggles to please her overbearing, narcissistic mother played by Barbara Hershey.

**Charlie Brown**—Charlie Brown is the lead character in Charles M. Schulz's classic *Peanuts* cartoons who is generally portrayed as feeling insecure and seeking acceptance. Charlie Brown's character contrasts with the somewhat narcissistic character of Lucy, and their relationship is sometimes used to illustrate the relationship between personality-disordered and non-personality-disordered people.

**Gaslight**—*Gaslight* is a 1944 MGM suspense thriller set in nineteenth-century London in which the villain, Gregory Anton (Charles Boyer), in an attempt to cover up his crimes, actively tries to convince his new wife, Paula (Ingrid Bergman), that she is losing her mind. *Gaslight* gave its name to the practice known as Gaslighting.

**Mommie Dearest**—*Mommie Dearest* is a 1981 biography of Hollywood Actress Joan Crawford, played by Faye Dunaway, who, according to the account in the movie, exhibited obsessive compulsive, borderline, and narcissistic traits.

**Schindler's List**—*Schindler's List* is a 1993 drama that chronicles the suffering of Jews in Nazi-occupied Poland during World War II and how Oskar Schindler, a German businessman, rescued over a thousand of them by employing them in his factories. The movie includes a striking portrayal of Amon Göth, a narcissistic SS officer and camp director, played by Ralph Fiennes.

**RESOURCE: www.outofthefog.com**

## NPD Support Groups and Links

Out of the Fog Support Forum—Support for family members and loved ones at Out of the Fog.

www.psychforums.com/narcissistic-personality/—Psychforums NPD Board

https://groups.yahoo.com/neo/groups/Adult-ChildrenOFNarcissits /info—Yahoo group for adult children of narcissistic parents.

http://p208.ezboard.com/bnarcissisticpersonalitydisoderfamilyforum— Narcissistic Personality Disorder Family Forum

Light's Blog—info sharing blog for survivors of narcissism.

It's All about Him—support site and discussion forum for women with NPD partners.

http://bnarcissisticabuserecovery.runboard.com/—Narcissistic Abuse Recovery Forum

**RESOURCE: www.outofthefog.com**

## Hotline Numbers

National Domestic Violence Hotline (in U.S.)—1-800-799-7233

National Sexual Assault Hotline–24/7 Hotline—1-800-656-4673

National Suicide Prevention Lifeline—1-800-273-TALK (8255)

# Notes

## Chapter 1: It All Began with an Apple

1. Psalm 42:5, New International Bible, Rainbow Studies, Inc.,1996.

2. Shannon Thomas, LCSW-S, *Healing From Hidden Abuse, A Journey Through the Stages of recovery from Psychological Abuse,* www.southlakecounseling.org, August 2016. Quote taken from excerpt on blog.

3. Katherine Schreiber, "Poison People," Psychology Today, June 2017, p.50-58, 88.

4. Sue Johnson, *Emotionally Focused Couple's Therapy with Trauma Survivors*, New York:

Guilford, 2002, 182.

5. Barbara Steffens, PhD, LPCC., and Marsha Means, MA., *Your Sexually Addicted Spouse: How Partners Can Cope and Heal*, New Horizons Press, Far Hills, NJ, 2009.10-11.

6. Ibid., 6-7

7. Ibid., 27.

8. Ibid., 30.

9. Dutch Sheets, *Intercessory Prayer*," Bethany House Publishers, Bloomington, MN, 55438,

1996. 181-185.

10. Sarah Young, *Jesus Today*, Thomas Nelson Publishers, Nashville, TN.

## Chapter 2: Nothing Is Wasted, Especially Your Suffering

1. Psalm 25:3A.

2. www.ncbi.nim.nih.gov/pmc/articles.PMC2669224/#.

3. Ibid.

4. Craig Malkin, PhD, *Rethinking Narcissism: The Bad—and the Surprising Good—About Feeling Special,* Harper Wave, New York, NY. 55.

5. Cai, Cambell, K.W., Kwan, Jean Twenge, J.M. Foster et.al. *"Incidence of Narcissism in the Current Culture,"* San Diego State University, research completed between 2002-2012.

6. Jean M. Twenge, PhD, *Narcissism Unleashed—Researchers Point to a Cultural Epidemic,* APS OBSERVER, Association for Psychological Science, December 10, 2013.

7. This document provides the appendices of The Narcissism Epidemic by Jean M. Twenge and W. Keith Campbell (Free Press, 2009). To buy the book, visit: http://www.amazon.com/o/ASIN/1416575987. For more information, return to the book website at http://www.narcissismepidemic.com

8. Jean M. Twenge, PhD, *Narcissism Unleashed—Researchers Point to a Cultural Epidemic,* APS OBSERVER, Association for Psychological Science, December 10, 2013.

9. Skerritt, Richard. *Tears and Healing: The Journey to the Light after An Abusive Relationship,* Dalkeith Press, 2005.

10. Joseph Burgo, www.YourTango.com, and writes for blogs.psychcentral.com/movies.

11. Dutton, D.J. and Painter, S.L., *Traumatic Bonding: The Development of Emotional Attachments in Battered Women and Other Relationships of Intermittent Abuse.* Victimology: An International Journal, pps 139-155.

12. Karla downing@karladowning.com, LMFT., www.ChangeMyRelationship.com

13. Gary Reese, *"Trauma Bond / Abusive Relationships,"* Feb. 25, 2013, www. The Hero's Journey, A healing Community forum, online.

14. Shahidi Arabi, *"Your Brain on Sex, Love, and Addiction: The Addiction to Bonding with Our Abuser,"* www.loveaddictiontreatment.com, April 27, 2014.

15. Stephen Arterburn and David Stoop, *Take Your Life Back—How to Stop Letting the Past and Other People Control You,* Tyndale House Publishers, Inc. 2016, 105.

## Chapter 3: A Darkened Mind

1. Matthew 13:15, Rainbow Edition of the New International Bible Version

2. John Bradshaw, *Bradshaw On: The Family, A Revolutionary Way of Self-Discovery*, 1988, Health Communications, Inc., Enterprise Center,3201 Southwest 15th Street, Deerfield Beach, Fl. 33442. 164.

3. Robert Subby, MA., and John Friel, PhD, "Codependency and Family Rules," 1984, Health Communications, Inc. Pompano Beach, Florida 33069.

4. John Bradshaw, *Bradshaw On: The Family*, ibid.

5. Ibid.

6. Jon Connelly, PhD, Rapid Resolution Therapy, Colorado Springs, CO. 2016.

7. Judith Lewis Herman, PhD, Trauma and Recovery: The Aftermath of Violence from Domestic Abuse to Political Terror, Basic Books, A Division of Harper Collins Publishers, 1992, 119.

8. Ibid., 119.

9. Ibid., 121.

10. Manning, Brennan, *Abba's Child: The Cry of the Heart for Intimate Belonging*, NavPress, 1994. pg.26.

11. 1 Timothy 6:10, NIV Rainbow Studies Edition, 1996.

12. American Psychiatric Association's Diagnostic and Statistical Manual, DSM-IV.

13. Malkin, C.W., *Clinical and Cultural Evidence to Support the Development of Narcissism*, Psychology Today, September 5, 2016.

14. THE COLLABORATIVE LONGITUDINAL PERSONALITY DISORDERS STUDY (CLPS): OVERVIEW AND IMPLICATIONS, Andrew E. Skodol, MD, John G. Gunderson, MD, M. Tracie Shea, PhD, MD, Leslie C. Morey, PhD, Charles A. Sanislow, PhD, Donna S. Bender, PhD, Carlos M. Grilo, PhD, Mary C. Zanarini, EdD, Shirley Yen, PhD, Maria E. Pagano, PhD, and Robert L. Stout, PhD. Journal of Personality Disorders, October 2005, 487-504

15. Rebecca Webber, *"The Real Narcissists,"* Psychology Today, September 05, 2016.

16. Lundy Bancroft, "*Why Does He Do That: Inside the Minds of Angry and Controlling Men,*" Berkley Press, September 3, 2003.

17. Matthew 12:34, NIV Rainbow Study Bible.

18. Malkin, C.W., *Clinical and Cultural Evidence to Support the Development of Narcissism,* Psychology Today, Sept. 05, 2016.

19. Rebecca Webber, "*The Real Narcissists,*" Psychology Today, September 05, 2016.

20. www.outofthefog.com

21. www.forbes.com/celebrities," The Global Celebrity 100-2016."

## Chapter 4: Treatment Interventions for NPD

1. Psalm 107:16-21, NIV Rainbow Study Bible, 1996.

2. The Diagnostic and Statistical Manual of the American Psychiatric Association, 2006.

3. Craig Malkin, PhD, "Is It Possible for the Narcissist in Your Life to Change?" Psychology Today, Sept. 20, 2013.

4. Ibid.

5. Ibid.

6. Sheen Ambardar, M.D., Chief Editor, and David Bienenfeld, et.al., www.Medscape.com, May 2016.

7. Martin Winkler, Web4Health, 08-23-08

8. Cynthia Lechan Goodman, M.Ed., &Barbara Leff, LCSW, "*The Everything Guide to Narcissistic Personality Disorder,*" Adams Media, Avon, Massachusetts, 2012, 49.

9. "NPD and the Connection to Eating Disorders": (Futures Palm Springs, Website for Professionals, 1-866-964-6379. TeQuesta, Fla., 33469.

10. PsychAlive: Psychology for Everyday, psych alive.org.

11. Russ Federman, PhD, ABPP, *The Relationship Between Bipolar Disorder and Narcissism: Distinctions, Similarity, and Synergy Between Narcissism and Bipolar Grandiosity,*" Psychology Today, Oct. 27, 2013.

12. Ibid., www.RussFederman.com

13. Mayo Clinic Staff writer, Patient Care and Information website—Nov. 18, 2014.

14. Cynthia Lechan Goodman, M.Ed. & Barbara Leff, LCSW, *"The Everything Guide to Narcissistic Personality Disorder,"* Adams Media, Avon, Massachusetts, 2012.

15. Sheen Ambardar, M.D., Chief Editor, and David Bienenfeld, et.al., www.Medscape.com, May 2016.

16. Cynthia Lechan Goodman, M.Ed., & Barbara Leff, LCSW, *"The Everything Guide to Narcissistic Personality Disorder,"* Adams Media, Avon, Massachusetts, 2012. p.70.

17. Ibid., 63-64.

18. Sheen Ambardar, M.D., Chief Editor, and David Bienenfeld, et.al., www.Medscape.com, May 2016.

19. Cynthia Lechan Goodman, M.Ed., & Barbara Leff, LCSW, *"The Everything Guide to Narcissistic Personality Disorder,"* Adams Media, Avon, Massachusetts, 2012.

20. Courtney Armstrong, M.Ed., *The Therapeutic "AHA!", Rapid Resolution Therapy,* W.W. Norton, New York, 2013, book jacket.

21. Big Book of Alcoholics Anonymous, Alcoholics Anonymous World Services, Inc., 3rd. Edition, 1976.

22. Mayo Clinic Staff writer, Patient Care and Information website—Nov. 18,2014.

23. Ibid.

## Chapter 5: Boundary Setting Skills with the Narcissist

1. Henry Cloud and John Townsend, *BOUNDARIES: When To say Yes and When to Say No—To take Control of Your Life,* Zondervan, Grand Rapids, Michigan, 1992.

2. Ibid.

3. Ibid.

4. Ephesians 5:28-29, New International Version Rainbow Bible, Rainbow Studies International, 1996.

5. "Setting Boundaries With A Narcissist," HealthResearchFunding.org, October 9, 2014, info@spartanlifecoach.com

6. Ibid.

7. Proverbs 4:23 NHEB.

8. Proverbs 26:24 ESV.

9. Becker, Steve, LCSW, CHT, Westfield, NJ, 2008—"Communicating With Narcissistic Personalities," www.powercommunicating.com

10. Ibid.

11. Ibid.

12. Ibid.

13. Ibid.

## Chapter 6: Practical Helps That Can't Hurt

1. Anonymous.

2. Shannon Thomas, LCSW-S, *Healing From Hidden Abuse, A Journey Through the Stages of Recovery from Psychological Abuse,* www.southlakecounseling.org, August 2016. Quote taken from excerpt on blog.

3. Sue Johnson, *Emotionally Focused Couple's Therapy with Trauma Survivors,* New York: Guilford, 2002, 182.

4. Barbara Steffens, PhD, LPCC., and Marsha Means, MA., *Your Sexually Addicted Spouse: How Partners Can Cope and Heal,* New Horizons Press, Far Hills, New Jersey, 2009.10-11.

5. Ibid., 6-7.

6. Ephesians 6:11-13. NIV Rainbow Study Bible, Rainbow Studies, Inc. 1996.

7. Joseph Burgo, *"Loving the Narcissist in Your Life,"* www.yourtango.com.

## Chapter 7: What to Do When What You've Tried Isn't Working

1. Matthew 11:28, NIV Rainbow Edition Study Bible, 1996.

2. David Smith, Pastor, Fairhaven Church, Dayton, OH, 45459, April 8, 2017.

3. Psalm 34:18, NIV Rainbow Edition.

4. Romans 12:17-19, NIV Rainbow Edition.

5. Romans 7:20, NIV Rainbow Edition.

6. Hebrews 7:27, NIV Rainbow Edition.

## Chapter 8: Surrender—Not My Will, Lord, but Yours Be Done

1. Joshua 1:9, NIV Rainbow Study Bible Edition, 1006.

2. Cynthia Lechan Goodman, M.Ed., & Barbara Leff, LCSW. *The Everything Guide to Narcissistic Personality Disorder*, Adams Media, Avon, Mas.,2012. 257.

3. W. Keith Campbell, PhD, *The Psychology of Narcissism*, TED Ed Lessons Worth Sharing, Blog.

4. Peter Gray, PhD, *Why is Narcissism Increasing Among Young Americans?*, Psychology Today, January 16, 2014.

5. Craig W. Malkin, PhD, *Clinical and Cultural Evidence to Support the Development of Narcissism*, Psychology Today, September 5, 2016.

6. Cynthia Lechan Goodman, MEd, & Barbara Leff, LCSW. *The Everything Guide to Narcissistic Personality Disorder*, Adams Media, Avon, Massachusetts, 2012. 255.

7. Luke 10:26-28, NIV Rainbow Study Bible Edition, 1996.

8. Philippians 4:13. ibid.

9. Colossians 3:12-14. ibid.

10. 1 Thessalonians 2:4. ibid.

11. 1 Peter 5:10-11. ibid.

12. Charles Stanley, *In Touch Devotional*, January 2017, 26.

13. Ibid. 26.

14. Luke 23:34a. ibid.

15. Luke 6: 27-28, ibid.

16. Dutch Sheets, "Intercessory Prayer," Bethany House Publishers, Bloomington, MN, 1996. 186.

17. Ibid., 186.

# NEWLIFE | Help in Life's Hardest Places

**Talking about the things no one else will, to bring healing to those who've lost hope**

*"I have been living with my secrets* for 30 plus years while failing time and again to stop and all the while them getting worse. For the first time I have learned more about why it is happening, developing an action plan to change, and creating a network of support."

*— Jack*
Intensive Workshop attendee

**NEW LIFE MINISTRIES EXISTS**
TO GO INTO LIFE'S HARDEST PLACES

*with you.*

**800-HELP-4-ME**
**NewLife.com**

When you or someone you love is in crisis, you need a trusted friend to walk alongside you—a helper who's been there and understands, but who also has the training and skill to offer practical help.

New Life Ministries, founded by Steve Arterburn, exists to go into life's hardest places with you.

For over 30 years, we've provided expert answers to people just like you on our call-in radio show, *New Life Live!* We also offer a host of other resources, Intensive Workshops, and referrals to a carefully selected network of counselors.

Visit NewLife.com today to see how we can help, or call 800-HELP-4-ME. We want to hear from you!

# About New Life Ministries

New Life Ministries, founded by Stephen Arterburn, began in 1988 as New Life Treatment Centers. New Life's nationally broadcast radio program, *New Life Live!*, began in early 1995. Women of Faith conferences, also founded by Stephen Arterburn, began in 1996. New Life's Counselor Network was formed in 2000, and TV.NewLife.com, the ministry's Internet-based television channel, was launched in 2014. New Life continues to develop and expand their programs and resources to help meet the changing needs of their callers and listeners.

Today, New Life Ministries is a nationally recognized, faith-based, broadcasting and counseling nonprofit organization providing ministry through radio, TV, their counseling network, workshops, support groups, and numerous written, audio, and video resources. All New Life resources are based on God's truth and help those who are hurting find and build connections and experience life transformation.

The *New Life Live!* radio program, still the centerpiece of the ministry, is broadcast on Christian radio stations in more than 150 markets. It can also be seen on several network and online channels.

New Life's passion is to reach out compassionately to those seeking emotional and spiritual health and healing for God's glory. New Life Ministries Resource Center receives thousands of calls each month from those looking for help.

For more information, visit newlife.com.

# About Stephen Arterburn

Stephen Arterburn, M.Ed., is the founder and chairman of New Life Ministries and host of the number-one nationally syndicated Christian counseling talk show *New Life Live!*, heard and watched by more than two million people each week on nearly two hundred stations nationwide. He is also the host of New Life TV, a web-based channel dedicated to transforming lives through God's truth, and he also serves as a teaching pastor in Indianapolis, Indiana.

Stephen is an internationally recognized public speaker and has been featured on national media venues such as *Oprah*, *Inside Edition*, *Good Morning America*, *CNN Live*, and *ABC World News Tonight*; in the *New York Times*, *USA Today*, *US News and World Report*; and even in *GQ* and *Rolling Stone* magazines. Stephen has spoken at major events for the National Center for Fathering, American Association of Christian Counselors, Promise Keepers Canada, the Lifewell Conference in Australia, and the Salvation Army, to name a few.

He is the bestselling author of books such as *Every Man's Battle* and *Healing Is a Choice*. With more than eight million books in print, Stephen has been writing about God's transformational truth since 1984. His ministry focuses on identifying and compassionately responding to the needs of those seeking healing and restoration through God's truth. Along with Dr. Dave Stoop, he edited and produced the number-one-bestselling *Life Recovery Bible*.

Stephen has degrees from Baylor University and the University of North Texas, as well as two honorary doctorates, and is currently completing his doctoral studies in Christian counseling. He resides with his family in Fishers, Indiana.

Stephen Arterburn can be contacted directly at SArterburn@newlife.com.

# About Patricia A. Kuhlman

Patricia A. Kuhlman, M.R.C., has been a seasoned clinical psychotherapist for nearly thirty years, during which she specialized in treating people whose hearts have been ravaged by trauma, abuse, brokenness, betrayal, and neglect. Having received a Master of Rehabilitation Counseling degree from Wright State University and significant Post Masters training in mental and emotional health from the University of Dayton, Ms. Kuhlman has been uniquely positioned to address the specific needs, life issues, and painful circumstances her clients bring. This preparation has equipped her for the challenging task of diagnosing and treating dually diagnosed clients. Her depth of practical knowledge and wisdom, along with vast life experience, has allowed her to quickly build safe, comfortable, engaging therapeutic relationships with individuals across the life span, as well as those involved in ministry, medicine, and corporate executives.

As a clinical psychotherapist and a born-again Christian, Patricia is able to address client needs and concerns using sound psychotherapeutic principles combined with a strong faith-based Christian foundation. Using this approach has enabled Ms. Kuhlman to be emotionally available while the Holy Spirit brings hope and healing, but also the freedom that accompanies personal life transformation.

Now in her fifteenth year as a member of New Life Ministry's national counseling network, Ms. Kuhlman has been a spiritual coach and facilitator for the nationally recognized ministry events, which include, Marriage Solutions; Lose It for Life; Women in the Battle; and Healing Is a Choice, led by well-known author and founder of *New Life Live!*, Stephen Arterburn.

It is Patricia's sincere desire for the reader to know that she holds fast to the belief that "God deliberately chooses broken people to be his vessels, and He calls us to be broken and poured out for others. We all follow a 'broken road' one step at a time to increasing Hope and Healing" (Ann Voskamp, *The Broken Way*, Zondervan, 2016). Ms. Kuhlman has lived and experienced much of what she has written about here. It is because she was once very broken and now has "eyes to see" that she believes God has used her here to help others along this broken road.

A lifetime resident of Ohio, Ms. Kuhlman currently resides in Dayton and is the proud mother of two young adult daughters. She can be contacted at www.taprootcentre.com.

At David C Cook, we equip the local church around the corner and around the globe to make disciples. Come see how we are working together—go to **www.davidccook.com**. Thank you!